The Many Deaths of Judas Iscariot

'An exciting and impressive text [which] will attract a lot of attention.'
Oliver Leaman

Is suicide a sin?

In his thirty-third year, Aaron Saari's elder brother – a sufferer from distressing mental illness – ended his own life by jumping off a rusting steel bridge into the Licking River in Kentucky, an action Christian teaching asserts will condemn him to Hell. Such personal tragedy could have turned this biblical scholar into a confirmed atheist – instead it cemented his faith.

Judas Iscariot has for centuries embodied the doctrine of God's abhorrence of suicide and is a powerful symbol of the cultural taboo, originating from Christian doctrine, which still clings to voluntary death. Yet, A.M.H. Saari argues, this ancient condemnation of Judas' death is unfounded: Judas is instead a literary invention of the Markan community meant to undercut the authority of the twelve, entering the Christian story c.70 CE through the Gospel of Mark.

In this bold, captivating and controversial book, the author combines his own intensely moving personal accounts with incisive scriptural analysis to challenge the reader to reassess what they think they know about Judas Iscariot and suicide.

Written with passion and clarity and consistently relevant to today's moral issues, this book is as much an ideal introduction to Biblical Studies for the general reader as it is essential reading for students, scholars, and anyone with an interest in Biblical Studies, Ancient Scripture and Theology.

A.M.H. Saari is an adjunct professor at Antioch University McGregor in Yellow Springs, Ohio, where he lives with his dog Guinness. A theologian, his interests lie primarily in the historical Jesus, Jesus in film, world religions and the philosophy of suicide. He still misses his brother.

The Many Deaths of Judas Iscariot

A meditation on suicide

A.M.H. Saari

Routledge
Taylor & Francis Group

LONDON AND NEW YORK

First published 2006 in the USA and Canada
by Routledge
270 Madison Avenue, New York, NY 10016

Simultaneously published in the UK
by Routledge
2 Park Square, Milton Park, Abingdon, Oxon OX14 4RN

Routledge is an imprint of the Taylor & Francis Group, an informa business

Typeset in Goudy MT by
RefineCatch Limited, Bungay, Suffolk
Printed and bound in Great Britain by
TJ International Ltd, Padstow, Cornwall

Library of Congress Cataloging in Publication Data
Saari, A. M. H.
    The many deaths of Judas Iscariot : a meditation on suicide / A. M. H.
Saari.
        p.   cm.
    Includes bibliographical references and index.
    1. Judas Iscariot.   2. Suicide–Religious aspects–
Christianity.   I. Title.
    BS2460.J8S27   2006
    226′.092–dc22   2005030669

British Library Cataloguing in Publication Data
A catalogue record for this book is available from the British Library

ISBN10: 0-415-39239-X (hbk)
ISBN10: 0-415-39240-3 (pbk)
ISBN10: 0-203-08748-8 (ebk)

ISBN13: 978-0-415-39239-6 (hbk)
ISBN13: 978-0-415-39240-2 (pbk)
ISBN13: 978-0-203-98748-0 (ebk)

For Stephen

Contents

Acknowledgments

First and foremost, I thank my brother Stephen for being in my life and, for an all too brief period, sharing himself with me. I am the man I am today because of his influence; he was riddled, for whatever reasons (if there are any discernible reasons), with a brutal and unforgiving disease. He took care of me the whole of my life, and for that I am eternally grateful.

To the faculty of Xavier University in Cincinnati, Ohio, for their undying confidence and belief in me. Had Xavier not been generous in both financial and intellectual support, this project, and my continued education, would not have been possible. Particular thanks must be extended to Dr Arthur Dewey, whose stalwart advice and leadership pushed me to make this the best project it could be. Also, my deepest gratitude to Father Kenneth Overberg, whose love of God and love of humanity contributed to my conversion to Christianity. In the days and weeks that followed Stephen's death, Father Overberg extended genuine love and support to me and my family. He is truly a man of God. To Holly Toensing, who made me realize that I do not have to write everything I know; we share the pain of loss and the gift of love. To Sarah Melcher, who challenged me to think deeply about the relationship between the Hebrew Bible and the Christian New Testament. Also, to Tom Planck, a fellow Xavier student and a true Christian. Tom knows how his presence helped me through the darkness; God bless you, Tom.

Most importantly, I thank my ex-wife Evangeline, who helped put me through graduate school and supported me, both emotionally and financially, as I wrote. No matter what happens between us, I will never forget what you have done to help me realize this goal, Vangie! To my father, Dr Jon Saari, who loves and supports his son, even when his son does very questionable things – his brilliance and belief in me is unwavering and unquestionable. To my mother, Peggy Saari, the greatest mother and greatest editor in the whole world. Had circumstances been different, she would have written this book; in many ways, like the other books we have worked on together, this is a shared effort. To my sister Melissa and my beautiful niece Caroline, who, during the writing of this book, lost a husband and father, respectively. I love you both, and no matter the time constraints and geographic distance, we shall always be family. To the whole Heiliger family, whose love for each other and God has made me realize the profound responsibility I have to humanity. (Particular thanks to the Reverend Dr Robert Heiliger, or "Papa Bob," my father-in-law and friend, whose theological insights have inspired me and given me strength.) To my close friends (particularly Clint Burmester, my God-brother, Thor Sage, and Nathan Summers), who oftentimes had to accept my prolonged absence and distracted mind because I was forever in the first century, thank you for believing in me and this project.

I extend my profoundest gratitude to Richard Stoneman, my publisher, and Amy Laurens, my editor. Had the amazing people at Routledge not taken a chance on a small-town boy in America, this book would never have seen the light of day. Thank you to my legal counsel, who wished to remain anonymous, but knows who she is. I also extend thanks to the many thinkers and authors upon whose work I developed this book. Although I may criticize and question their contentions, I stand upon the shoulders of giants. Particular thanks are given to John Dominic Crossan, Arthur Dewey, Raymond Brown, A. Alvarez, Arthur J. Droge, James D. Tabor, Elaine Pagels, John Meier, W.H.C. Frend, William Klassen and James Carroll. May this book, in some small way, contribute to the never-ending search for the truth.

Finally, to the families of Elliott Smith and Spalding Gray, who both lost loved ones to voluntary death during the writing of this book. I have chosen to make my own story public; they, unfortunately, did not have that choice. I hope they are able to find peace and comfort knowing that they are not alone.

Aaron Saari
Yellow Springs
January 2006

List of abbreviations

Cor	Corinthians
Deut	Deuteronomy
Ex	Exodus
Gal	Galatians
GPet	The Gospel of Peter
Isa	The Book of Isaiah
Jer	Jeremiah
Lk	The Gospel of Luke
Mk	The Gospel of Mark
Mt	The Gospel of Matthew
NT	New Testament
Ps	Psalms
Rom	Romans
Sam	Samuel
Thess	Thessalonians
Wis	The Wisdom of Solomon
Zec	Zechariah
//	passage parallel to

All Greek New Testament passages are from the Nestle-Aland *Greek–English New Testament*, Stuttgart: Deutsche Bibelgesellschaft, 1981.

Unless noted otherwise, English translations of New Testament passages are from *The Complete Gospels: Annotated Scholar's Version*, 3rd edn, Sonoma: Polebridge Press, 1994.

English translations of the Hebrew Bible are from The Jewish Publishing Society *Tanakh*, 1985.

Excerpts from Q are cited by the parallel passage in Luke.

Part I
Life

Prologue

For my soul is full of troubles,
and my life draws near to Sheol.
I am counted among those who go down to the Pit,
I am like those who have no help,
like those forsaken among the dead,
like the slain that lie in the grave,
like those whom you remember no more,
for they are cut off from your hand.
You have put me in the depth of the Pit,
in the regions dark and deep.
Your wrath lies heavy upon me,
and you overwhelm me with all your waves.

Psalm 88:3–7

On 12 October 2003 I stood on a rusting steel bridge overlooking the Licking River in Covington, Kentucky, the Cincinnati skyline visible behind me, as cars sped past and the dirty river water flowed lazily forty feet below. My wife Evangeline stood silently beside me as I read the eighty-eighth psalm from my Oxford Annotated Bible, the only time in my life I had used that particular Bible, or any Bible as a matter of fact, for spiritual comfort rather than academic study. At times, presumably when the traffic lights halted oncoming cars, my voice was all that could be heard, save the subtle sounds of water lapping against the river banks. The sky, which had begun the day a sharp, flinty grey, was a brilliantly clear blue. It had taken me two months to decide if I would make the journey to Kentucky, and as I was finally standing on the bridge the moment seemed anti-climactic.

I have made the drive to Cincinnati from my hometown of Yellow Springs, Ohio, thousands of times in my life. Born and raised in Ohio, I have spent a majority of my twenty-seven years living either in

Cincinnati or Yellow Springs. Shortly before my twenty-fourth birthday I bought a home in the sleepy hamlet of Clifton, not five miles from my parents' home in Yellow Springs. For over a year I had been making the seventy-mile drive from Clifton to the campus of Xavier University, located in Cincinnati, where I was taking classes in pursuit of my master of arts degree in theology. Mostly I enjoyed the drive; like many Americans, I found that often the only peace I could find away from the hustle and bustle of life was in my car. This fall day was different, however; when I pulled away from the driveway I began the journey along my own personal *Via Dolorosa*.

My heart was heavy with memories as the familiar terrain passed outside the car window, and as I neared the destination I wondered if I was in fact traveling the same route my older brother, Stephen, had driven exactly one year earlier. The written instructions on how to get to the Veterans' Memorial Bridge were sitting on my coffee table at home, but the previous evening's conversation with my mother was still fresh in my mind. After finding a parking space right next to the bridge (just as Mom told me I would), my wife and I walked onto the bridge and made our way half-way down its length. I looked down into the waters Stephen had successfully used to take his own life on a Saturday in his thirty-third year.

Suicide and mental illness were nothing new to me when the police chief's phone call came on a Wednesday night in October of 2002. My paternal uncle, Fred, had killed himself when I was a year old; this detail was kept from me until I learned about it by accident from my brother's girlfriend nine years later. Instead of telling me the truth, my family said that Fred had died of cancer, a lie I believed until I was sixteen. That year I questioned my mother about Fred's death and she finally told me the truth, but refused to divulge any details; she told me my father should be the one to relate the entire story. I tried to talk to my father but he avoided the question; I was confused as to why it was such a big secret. That same year, when I was a junior in high school, I was afforded a unique opportunity to break the silence. I wrote a one-act play that was performed by the high-school drama club. I insisted that I be cast in the lead role; it was a desperate attempt to get my father to talk to me about his brother's death. I believed that art, in this case, might imitate life. It is chilling how correct I was in the end.

In the play I portrayed a young boy wrestling with whether or not to read the suicide note left for him by his brother. The boy's conscience, also a character in the play, assures the boy that the death of his brother was his, the boy's, fault. In the end, the boy drops the unopened suicide note into the open grave of his brother, telling his conscience that he would rather have his memories than insight into his brother's pain. Stephen never saw the play, but he heard about it; on a hot August day, drinking beer I was too young to legally imbibe, he promised me he would never kill himself. I reciprocated the promise, but I never had to deal with schizophrenia; Stephen did.

During my senior year of high school I was cast as Pontius Pilate in our production of *Jesus Christ Superstar*. I had been an avid fan of the rock opera since I was a child; a cherished early memory is of sitting on my sister Melissa's bed, asking her if the man counting along with the music was nailing Jesus to the cross. No, she told me, Pilate is whipping Jesus before he is crucified. The image of that event both fascinated and horrified me. I could not understand why anyone would want to treat another person with such cruelty; but, thinking with a young child's mind, I concluded that no one was punished unless it was deserved. Without realizing it, my four-year-old mind had internalized the theology of retribution: God punishes only those who have sinned. One could say that I first learned of the Passion of Jesus through the music of Andrew Lloyd Webber and the lyrics of Timothy Rice. Hearing the story from Judas Iscariot's point of view has had an indelible influence upon me and my spiritual development. Although I did not know it at the time – at least, I would not have been able to express myself as I can today – I felt drawn to Judas because he was an outsider who desperately wanted to be included. Judas in *Jesus Christ Superstar* is the odd man out, the one to whom no one wants to listen. From a young age, I felt that Jesus was wholly unknowable; Judas seemed to be a lot like me.

Raised as a good Western secular humanist, the only thing I knew as a small child about Jesus was that he was born at Christmas so Santa could bring me presents, and that he died at Easter so the Easter Bunny could bring me candy. I thought it was very nice of him to do so, but I wondered how he could have achieved so many important things when there were so few months between Christmas and Easter. It is funny, but not necessarily in a humorous way, how we approach the Christian story and the things we assume and internalize; the details we think we know are often the products of our own imagination. Over the decades, much of that internalization has caused me a great deal of pain.

When I left home at eighteen, I felt that I had been liberated from my parents' control. Like most young kids let loose at university, I rebelled against everything I knew. My rebellion, though, was unique: choosing courses, I decided to major in religion – a direct challenge to my father, an avowed atheist. I began studying the historical Jesus, entrenching myself in the first century in an attempt to discover what had been kept from me my whole life: knowledge of Christianity. I felt transformed by the works of John Dominic Crossan, Elaine Pagels and Raymond Brown. I realized for the first time in my life that I yearned for God, but I did not have the spiritual acumen to express this need.

I approached God the way I approached everything in my life, with my intellect. I searched for God in the pages of academic texts, sought out God in theories, commentaries and works of theology. But I remained unsatisfied, unfulfilled. I did not feel the wonder and joy produced by God's presence, a wonder and joy described with elegance and beauty by the writers of the Tanakh (the Hebrew Bible) and the Gospels. In reality, I did not know how to love. I hated myself and I thought God should turn that hate into love, but my anger and alienation kept me from approaching God with love and humility. Because I did not know how to love, I did not know how to receive love, and I failed to see God.

As my university years passed, I went through the expected rites of passage. The most dramatic result was that I no longer identified myself as an atheist. I was smart enough to know that I did not know; I tempered my arrogance and accepted the fact that God could very well exist. Although I would not admit it to anybody, I wanted more than anything for God to exist. I begged God to reveal God's self to me. I sought God through books, music, drugs, alcohol, sex, conversation and almost every other avenue I could think of. But I did not find what I was looking for. Exhausted, dejected and angry, I told myself that God was not for everyone; I made excuses for my lack of spirituality. I told myself that I was too smart to be duped by the lies. In reality, I was too arrogant to see that God was there all the while, just not in the way that my preconceived notions had made me expect.

Stephen and Melissa have a different father than I. My mother divorced when Stephen was about four, and within a short time she remarried. When Stephen was six years, six months and six days old, I was born. From the time of my earliest memories, Stephen was my whole world. I thought he was the epitome of cool and I idolized him in every way. I wanted to wear his clothes and hang out with his friends; I made every attempt to emulate him. Painfully shy but devastatingly handsome, Stephen was well liked by others, but he did not know how to handle attention. He spent a lot of time at home; after my sister left for college, when I was six, Stephen and I were the only kids in the house. Until he was sixteen and became involved with his first real girlfriend, Stephen spent most of his time with me. We built model trains, rode skateboards and spent hours racing electric slot-cars in the basement. To this day, the mixed smells of hot copper and plastic remind me of weekends in the cool of the basement, listening to songs by AC/DC and holding 500-lap slot-car races.

Even after graduating from high school and moving into an apartment of his own, sixty miles away, Stephen made it a point to stay in my life. Imagine a nineteen-year-old man with a live-in girlfriend inviting his twelve-year-old brother to stay for a whole week. That was Stephen. He made me a priority; being my brother was part of his identity. He taught me about sex, took me to get my ear pierced and bought me my first illegal beer. He told me about his hopes and dreams, fears and aspirations, and beseeched me to learn from his mistakes. By the time I was seventeen, my brother was my best and oldest friend.

When I began my first year of university studies, Stephen was finishing his final year at the same institution. He had gone through some difficult times in his early twenties, mostly casting about from dead-end job to dead-end job, involved in a series of bad relationships. After several years of this, Stephen went back to school, first at a community college and then at a well-respected four-year liberal arts university. I had decided at a very early stage to go to the same school, about a year before Stephen began attending, but his presence just solidified my decision. I began my matriculation elated that Stephen and I would be college men together, but I respected Stephen's space and autonomy. I knew that he had established a life for himself there, and I did not want to encroach upon it.

Still, we spent a good deal of time together, mostly drinking beer and discussing ideas. One of my fondest memories is of watching *The Ten Commandments* on a small television in his dorm room while talking about the nature of God. Stephen, like me, yearned for something greater, and he thought he had found it in the academic world. He wanted to be a literature professor, specializing in the work of Norman Mailer. It was the first time I had ever heard him speak optimistically about the future. I shared with him my newly discovered love: the study of religion. He listened to me as I recounted the historical developments of the ancient world, where gods did battle with one another and covenants were written in stone. We imagined that bold and dynamic lives lay in front of us. The year was 1995.

Stephen was diagnosed with schizophrenia in November of 1998. The years of his descent are too painful and too private to recount. In 1998, however, the years of decline came to a head. He suffered a mental breakdown, attempting a suicide that was more a cry for help than a concerted effort to take his life, but the reality was still the same: Stephen tried to kill himself. I was shocked and saddened by the development. I desperately wanted to reach out to him, but I did not know how. I remember looking at him in the hospital, his face drawn and tired, his eyes vacant and empty, and just feeling relief that after three years of watching him become a man none of us recognized, there was finally a name to associate with the behavior: schizophrenia. Stephen left the hospital after a mandatory observation period, and moved into my parents' house. He never moved out.

At the time Stephen was discharged from the hospital, we were told by mental health experts to treat him as though nothing was different; it was our task to help him establish a routine. Stephen was placed on heavy medication, and his condition was treated with a code of silence; we told no one in the family, not even my sister, what had happened. Stephen was mortified and embarrassed by the direction his life had taken. I can only imagine what it was like for Stephen, adjusting to the starkness and finality of his situation. He knew he could never work again, never live on his own and never have a lasting, meaningful relationship with a woman.

Under my parents' roof and under the influence of psychotropic drugs, Stephen's life became strictly regimented within a matter of weeks. He awoke at the same time every morning, had his coffee, took a shower (which he would only do if someone were in the house), watched television, went to the grocery store, helped prepare the meals and ended his day sitting mutely in front of the television. This was Stephen's routine, with subtle changes and refinements developed over the course of several years, until the last day of his life, when he was finally freed from the confines of the desperate situation.

After Stephen's breakdown, the holidays passed in a quiet confusion. I watched my brother – who seemed calmer and more relaxed than I had seen him in years, but somehow fundamentally different – adjust to his new reality. I was bursting with desire to ask Stephen questions, to tell him I was sorry for not being there when things were really dark for him, but I did not know how. He seemed so different to me, as if an alien was living inside the body of my brother. At the time I made excuses for why I could not reach out to Stephen. I told myself that the holidays were stressful enough for him without my asking questions about the suicide attempt. I decided to wait until after the first of the year; with a new year, I told myself, I can begin anew with my new brother.

Unfortunately, when the first of the year came my family was faced with another ordeal. My father was diagnosed with a massive brain tumor that required immediate surgery. Once again our lives fundamentally changed, and my father's illness overshadowed that of Stephen. Given that my father – a muscle-bound man who at fifty-two had the physique of a bodybuilder – lay in a hospital bed thirty pounds lighter than he had been the previous week, it was easy to treat Stephen as though we were all experiencing the same reality. Thoughts that my father could die pushed questions about Stephen's well-being to the wayside. In many ways, I was just relieved that Stephen was on medication and under our watchful eye. I no longer feared for his life the way I had in November. My father's health, on the other hand, was touch-and-go. I was terrified that I was going to lose him. Our lives were overtaken by his illness.

After the first surgery, my father was sent home to my mother's care. Late one night, my father fell out of bed, with a seizure. He had to endure another major operation to relieve the edema. He fell briefly into a coma, and when he awoke he was blind. This condition persisted for months, until one day his sight began to re-emerge gradually. For two years my family – Stephen included – went on seemingly endless trips to doctors' appointments, radiation treatments and checkups. As a result of excellent care and his indefatigable spirit, my father recovered. He has regained a good deal of his sight and lives a comfortable, albeit limited life to this day.

As the turn of the millennium came and went, we tried to adjust our lives to new realities. Stephen's illness and Dad's changed health were not the only things that happened. My sister Melissa gave birth to a daughter, Caroline. Our family's joy soon turned to sorrow, however; Melissa's husband, Dave, was also diagnosed with a brain tumor. Unfortunately, Dave did not fare as well as my father. During the writing of this book, Dave passed away. More tragedy had struck my family during this turbulent time. My paternal grandmother was ravaged by Alzheimer's and, after a brief struggle, died. My paternal grandfather's second wife, Lorraine, suffered a brain hemorrhage before my very eyes and died less than two weeks later. Life was not all suffering, however: eight years after beginning my education, I graduated from college; my best friend, Clint, fathered a son; one beautiful June day, my longtime girlfriend became my wife. Life, as it always does, went on despite hardships and blessings. I did what I could to adjust to all these changes, all the while wondering where God was and why there was so much pain levied upon my family.

Before 12 October 2002, the saddest fact of my life, without a doubt, was that the once intensely close relationship I had enjoyed with Stephen was gone forever. When I learned that Stephen was schizophrenic, I put the painful memories behind me. The hurtful and sometimes horrible person he had become was the result of a brutal and unforgiving disease. I accepted this with relative ease, and forgave him for his behavior. I also accepted that I could never expect anything from Stephen again, but that I had to love him as much as I ever had, if not more. This experience taught me a great deal about the nature of love: to love someone completely and fully while getting little or nothing in return is difficult. I would be lying if I said that I was always successful in this endeavor, but I did the best I could.

I spent time with Stephen, but – as anyone who has attempted to maintain a relationship with a schizophrenic will tell you – it is impossible to have a deep, meaningful conversation. Sometimes it can feel as though you are casting about, drowning in a sea of uncertainty, alienation and regret. By a certain point, the capacity for genuine connection with a schizophrenic is gone. Perhaps it is overly simplistic to blame my inability to connect with Stephen exclusively on the disease. By the time it became clear that Dad's recovery was permanent, it seemed too late for me to ask my brother questions about his suicide attempt. It seemed futile to express sorrow and regret for my actions during his years of darkness. To my mind, Stephen had adjusted to his new life. I did not want to upset him by asking painful questions. For his part, Stephen played the role of big brother in every way he could. Every so often we would go to movies together, talk about his beloved NASCAR races or the most recent episodes of *Survivor*. He came to my house and helped me tend the garden and mow the lawn; we changed the oil on the riding lawnmower together. Sometimes we would rent a movie and share a beer. But mostly, Stephen retreated into his own world, a world ruled by obsessive routine. He truly was a prisoner of his mind.

In many ways, I lost Stephen three times. I lost him when his illness caused his behavior to become so severe that I was forced to cut him out of my life. I lost him again when it became clear that the medicated and diagnosed Stephen, while calmer and less volatile, was nothing like the brother with whom I had grown up. And, of course, I lost him for good when he took his own life. But before Stephen left me forever, he gave me one last gift. Although emotionally distant and fearful of large crowds, he was in my wedding party and had a central role in the ceremony. Right before Evangeline and I joined hands to begin our wedding vows, I gave Stephen a hug in front of the guests and told him I loved him. He returned the hug and said he loved me too; it was the last time he ever uttered those words to me.

When Stephen was still alive I accepted the fact that he was changed forever, but I had a hard time dealing with feelings of guilt over his schizophrenia. Until the day his body was pulled from the Ohio River, where it had washed up after four days, I thought the greatest theological dilemma I would have to face in my life was why God had given my brother a devastating mental illness. I questioned why a gentle, loving man was being forced to live an existence in which he was imprisoned by his routines. I did not understand how it was that I was able to marry, go to school, maintain friendships and experience the wonders and joys of the world while my older brother was denied the basic components of a normal life.

I was wracked by guilt over this reality. Not one week before Stephen's death, I was crushed almost completely by feelings of agony. As my wife watched in helpless horror, I fell onto our bed, curled into the fetal position and sobbed violently. I cursed, challenged and even tried to strike a barter with God. I begged that I be the one limited and imprisoned by illness and that Stephen be given a life of happiness and companionship; I vowed my undying devotion and belief in return. Although I had spent much of my academic life studying about God, I had no idea how a just God could allow something such as this to happen. When I awoke the next morning, still myself and Stephen still ill, I gave up any chance of ever believing in God. I remained an agnostic, but I scoffed at the idea of a benevolent, loving God.

After we received word that Stephen had killed himself, my entire epistemology and system of belief were transformed. For the first time in my life I felt the complete and total presence of God. In what was my darkest hour I was given the strength to make arrangements for Stephen's remains, organize and minister his memorial service, and establish a charitable fund in his name. I was filled with a strength so unshakable that I knew it could not come from me alone; I had dealt with tragedy and pain for several years and was accustomed to moments of need and trial. I knew the limits of my personal capacity. But Stephen's death had been the one event I always feared would push me over the edge, the reality that would be too much to assimilate. Some-how, though, I did not fall and I did not break. Instead, I walked away from that edge and placed even greater burdens upon my shoulders. I choose to call the source of that unbelievable strength God. To regard it as otherwise seemed – and seems – counter-intuitive to me. There is no other explanation, and for the first time in my life my rational mind did not try to convince me that belief in God is irrational. Something intangible inside my being resonated with the truth of God's presence. At the moment when an agnostic should become an atheist, I was filled with love of and for God.

I am often wary of relating this anecdote to others. Certainly I am not embarrassed to believe in God, and I do not question the validity of my beliefs. However, I have found that people mean very different things by the word "God." When asked about my personal beliefs, I in return wonder about the inquisitor's personal theology. What will an answer in the affirmative indicate to him or her? Will my assent be a tacit approval of a damaging and non-holistic theology? Will my own beliefs be subject to interrogation and probing, only to be rejected upon the basis of predetermined criteria? What does someone really want to know about me when he or she asks if I believe in God? These questions are very important to me, because I was led to God as a result of my brother's death. Of my brother's suicide.

I believed at the time of Stephen's death, as I do now, that his suicide was an act of victory. He was able to overcome the demons and take control of his life before he was pulled inextricably into the abyss. In hindsight, the signs that Stephen was contemplating his own end could not have been more clear. Already withdrawn, he retreated into himself with an even greater assiduity in the months before his death; he spent countless hours in front of the television and showed less and less interest in engaging on any personal level. He began talking to himself in different voices, although he did this in the privacy of his room, and my family could not be certain at the time that we heard what we thought we heard. After his death these signs seemed to be crystal-clear, but when he was alive, these behaviors were simply part of Stephen's reality, and we did not want to upset him by querying them. Clearly, his pain proved to be too much and Stephen was able to end it on his own terms. I cannot help but see the hand of God in this event.

After Stephen's death my greatest theological question was no longer why my brother was afflicted with mental illness while I was perfectly healthy, but why suicide is seen as a sin against God in the Judeo-Christian tradition. Certainly, I reasoned, God would not have wanted Stephen to spend fifty years living in a mental hospital, drugged and watching reruns of *Leave it to Beaver*. Stephen's act was not one of cowardice but of courage, I said at his memorial service; the greatest thing one can do, I pontificated, paraphrasing Jesus, is to lay down his life for his friends. I felt Stephen had done that. He saved those who loved him, and more importantly himself, from decades of unnecessary pain, required not by God but by asinine social conventions that value quantity of life over quality of life.

Over the next few months, as the shock turned to numbness, the numbness to ache, the ache to acquiescence, I thought quite a bit about Judas Iscariot. Often I was flooded with memories in which Christians with whom I had spoken during my lifetime justified their abhorrence of suicide by connecting it to Judas. Sinners get what they deserve, these people said: Just look at Judas. What I could not understand, however, was the source from which these Christians were getting this information. Many spoke as though all the gospels relate that Judas kills himself, when in fact only Matthew does. A completely different death – one not by suicide, but a curious headlong fall – is related in the Acts of the Apostles. The other gospels are silent on the death of Judas. How then, I wondered, do so many Christians emerge with such a clear and passionate view regarding Judas Iscariot? Determined to learn more, I began to read as much as I could on the subject. After several months of study I decided that my upcoming master's thesis would focus on the deaths of Judas and an attempt to make sense of them. What resulted is the following examination.

There are two audiences for this book. The first is the general reader, Christian and non-Christian alike. We have all, to one degree or another, internalized the story of Judas Iscariot, and in most cases we believe things that are not found in the narratives themselves. I attempt to unpack the Judas story and present it within an historical framework. In pursuit of this goal, I explore not only the figure of Judas but the issue of suicide in the ancient world. The second audience is scripture scholars. Sections of the book are quite detailed and discuss various scholarly theories in depth. Often I use personal anecdotes to introduce issues discussed in chapters. The anecdotes are meant to underscore how pervasive the assumptions are that we make in society, and how what we think we know about Judas, and therefore about those who kill themselves, has no scriptural basis.

When we conclude our investigation, it is my hope that the reader will have a deeper appreciation for the figure of Judas Iscariot, and a greater understanding of exactly what the Hebrew Bible and Christian New Testament say, and do not say, about suicide. Although it is the intent of this investigation to begin at the earliest levels of the written Christian tradition and trace the evolution of the Judas narrative from Mark to Luke–Acts, we must in fact begin with the fourth-century writer Augustine, Bishop of Hippo in North Africa. Many of the ideas Christians have about suicide and about the figure of Judas come not from the scriptures themselves, but from thinkers such as Augustine. Therefore, to introduce the reader to the pertinent questions we shall be examining, it is necessary to begin in the fourth century before we can turn our attention back to the first.

1   The legacy of Augustine

For it is clear that if no one has a private right to kill even a guilty man (and no law allows this), then certainly anyone who kills himself is a murderer, and is the more guilty in killing himself the more innocent he is of the charge on which he has condemned himself to death. We rightly abominate the act of Judas, and the judgment of truth is that when he hanged himself he did not atone for the guilt of his detestable betrayal but rather increased it, since he despaired of God's mercy and in a fit of self-destructive remorse left himself no chance of a saving repentance. How much less right has anyone to indulge in self-slaughter when he can find in himself no fault to justify such a punishment! For when Judas killed himself; he killed a criminal, and yet he ended his life guilty not only of Christ's death, but also of his own; one crime led to another. Why then should a man, who has done no wrong, do wrong to himself? Why should he kill the innocent in putting himself to death, to prevent a guilty man from doing it? Why should he commit a sin against himself to deprive someone else of the chance?

Augustine of Hippo[1]

Augustine of Hippo is a fascinating figure. Born of a Christian mother and a pagan father in the small North African town of Tagaste in 354 CE, Augustine was trained as a rhetorician in the cosmopolitan center of Carthage. Early in his life he was attracted to Manichaeism, an esoteric branch of Gnosticism that highlighted a sharp division between the rational and the corporeal, the soul and the body. By his own admission Augustine did not travel up the hierarchical ladder, as he would years later as a Christian, and he was left unsatisfied by the metaphysical solutions the religion offered. When his career as a lecturer took him from Rome to Milan, Augustine became interested in Neoplatonism, particularly the works of Plotinus. As he studied this philosophical system, Augustine found satisfactory answers about the origin of evil, the nature of God and the substance of the soul. Augustine was not yet a Christian, but the influence of this philosophy would leave an indelible mark on his future faith. In many ways, Christianity has never been the same since Augustine applied Neoplatonic ideas to theology.

Augustine's famous conversion took place in Milan, under the tutelage of Ambrose (339–397), Bishop of Milan – and, according to Augustine himself, as a result of the incessant prayers of his mother. Agonizing in a garden over his lack of faith and inability to renounce worldly pursuits for a spiritual life, Augustine heard the voice of a child crying out to him "Take it and read, take it and read."[2] Opening a Bible at Paul's Epistle to the Romans, Augustine read: "Go home and sell all that belongs to you. Give to the poor, and so the treasure you have shall be in heaven; then come back and follow me" (Rom 13:13–14). His life was forever changed, as was Christianity.

We must not underestimate Augustine's importance to Christianity, particularly Catholicism. Church historian William C. Placher writes, "More than anyone else, Augustine shaped Western Theology and made it different from the traditions of the East. For the Western half of the church throughout the Middle Ages his authority stood second only to that of Scripture."[3] In the case of Judas Iscariot, as I shall attempt to show over the course of the following chapters, Augustine's authority superseded that of scripture. So, what does Augustine say about Judas and what is his scriptural evidence?

The quotation from Augustine at the opening of this chapter presents us with all the questions we must answer in order to understand negative attitudes to suicide up till now. Augustine equates suicide with homicide, making them one and the same. We must ask if this syllogism existed prior to Augustine, in both the Greco-Roman tradition and the world of Judaica from which Christianity evolved. Judas' act of suicide does not atone for his act of betrayal, rather it compounds his guilt. Here two important questions arise that are central to our investigation: First, has Judas' "detestable act" always been considered a betrayal? That is, does the evidence we have from the scriptures and other relevant documents point to a univocal understanding of Judas that has been consistent throughout the millennia? Second, is there evidence to support Augustine's claim that suicide compounds the guilt of a criminal or, as he states later in the quotation, introduces sin into an otherwise unblemished character? In other words, is suicide really a sin? Finally, does Augustine unequivocally denounce all self-imposed deaths as sinful? If so, how does the position relate to the venerated community of saints, many of whom died the death of a martyr?

To wade through this morass of issues properly, we must start at the earliest level. As our interest lies in the suicide of Judas, it is best to begin with the earliest material available, or not available as the case may be, about Judas. In the following chapter we shall look at the letters of Paul and the hypothetical Q document, both of which date from the middle of the first century, approximately two decades after the death of Jesus. Once we see what these sources have to say about Judas, we can begin an investigation of the canonical gospels, comparing and contrasting our findings, all the while keeping in mind the dire condemnation given by our old friend, Augustine of Hippo.

2 The earliest levels of the written Christian tradition: Paul and Q

It is important to emphasize that for the early Christian community the two key actors in the arrest, trial, and death of Jesus were Jesus and God. What they did was central; what others did is framework. To focus on what Judas might have done or not done and, most important, to spend energy on decrying what he did is to miss the point of it all.

William Klassen[1]

It has been said that Christianity could have been created without Jesus, but it most certainly could not exist without Paul. While such a sentiment may not be popular, and may even be construed by some as heresy, there is much truth in the statement. The bulk of the New Testament (NT) is either written by Paul (the genuine Pauline epistles), attributed to Paul (the psuedoepigrapha, epistles written by followers of Paul and attributed to him), or is about Paul (the Acts of the Apostles). As the gospels are most commonly read through the lens of John, that is, with the Johannine theology (theology of John) and Christology (ideas about Christ)[2] in mind, so too the thoughts of Paul indelibly have shaped Christianity. Yet, to those who wish to find the Jesus of history, Paul offers precious little evidence.

If we had only the writings of Paul with which to construct a picture of the historical Jesus, all we would know is that he was crucified and died. This fact does not diminish Paul's contribution to Christianity (for Paul was not interested in the Jesus of history but in the Christ of faith), yet it does pose a stumbling block for the historian who wishes to discern the earliest levels of the Jesus tradition. Saul of Tarsus, known after his conversion on the Damascus road as Paul, was a Pharisaic Jew,[3] an accomplished rhetorician, a Roman citizen and a Christian convert. He did not write a gospel (literally "good news");

rather he wrote letters, in Greek, to communities he had either started or had visited as a spiritual guide.

Paul gave these communities advice on how to conduct themselves awaiting the Parousia, or return of the Anointed. Paul is a frustratingly complex figure, for the Paul who emerges in the epistles is much different from the Paul presented in the Acts of the Apostles.[4] While the present treatment is not concerned with discovering the Paul of history, it is important to note that Paul interprets Jesus in a specific way: for Paul, the truth of God revealed through Jesus focuses on Jesus' death and subsequent resurrection; all else is of secondary importance. As such, Paul is less a Jesus-follower and more a member of an early Christ cult, distinctions I shall make more clear as our examination unfolds.

CAN GOD BETRAY? AN EXAMINATION OF THE GREEK WORD *PARADIDŌMI*

As noted above, the only historical detail Paul relates about Jesus is that of the crucifixion. Despite this, Paul does discuss an event that is central to our topic, the "handing over" of Jesus to the authorities. The earliest reference in all Christian writings to Jesus being handed over comes in Paul's first letter to the Corinthians, a largely Gentile (non-Jewish) community in Corinth, Greece. The letter is an excellent example of Pauline concerns: he adjures the members to cease their divisive ways and strive for unity in the face of the imminent Parousia. While an explication of the epistle is beyond the scope of our topic, it is necessary to understand what was important to Paul and how he bolsters his argument.

It appears that the Corinthian community was socially mixed, as there is a reference to a "few" wealthy members (1 Cor 1:26–28) who were perhaps the ones who ate and drank to their heart's content while the other members, possibly still at work, arrived at the meetings later and were forced to go without nourishment and libations (1 Cor 11:17–22). Paul, in typical rhetorical fashion, appeals to authority to make his point: he cites the example of Jesus and what the purpose of the meal is to be. "I received from the lord the same thing I gave over [*paredōka*] to you, that on the night when he was handed over [*paredidōto*], the Lord Jesus took bread . . ." (1 Cor 11:23; my translation, my italics) and performed the Eucharistic meal. If one were to look at this passage in the Revised Standard Version, the New English Bible or the Jerusalem Bible, the term I have translated as "he was handed over"

would be rendered "he was betrayed." The Greek root for both *paredōka*
and *paredidōto*[5] is the same word, *paradidōmi*.

One may ask why the same word, albeit in different forms, is translated so differently. What type of understanding would emerge if we
translated the passage as "I received from the Lord the same thing I
betrayed to you"? Perhaps the Greek word has two distinct meanings
that are used interchangeably, depending on context? To understand if
this is true, we must look at how the word is used in extant Greek
manuscripts before we can return to the biblical texts. Only then
can we responsibly establish why the translation I argue for is more
accurate than what is commonly found in English New Testaments;
therefore a brief discussion of etymology is warranted here. Much of
what follows relies upon the scholarship of William Klassen.[6]

Understanding the etymology

The form of Greek used in the NT is known as koine Greek, or
common Greek. Classical Greek, the form used by traditional Greek
philosophers and historians, is more structured and regimented, but
there is definitely a relationship between the two. We should therefore
look at how the term is used both in classical and common Greek.
First, the standard definitions of *paradidōmi* in classical Greek, found
in the Liddell and Scott lexicon, are:

1   To give, hand over to another, transmit, such as virtues from
     teacher to students, documents, give up an argument, etc.
2   To give a city or person into another's hands, esp. as a hostage or an
     enemy with the collational notion of "treachery, betray."
3   To give oneself up to justice.
4   To hand over legends, opinions, doctrines.

The second definition is very important. As Klassen points out, no
texts can be found in all of classical Greek in which *paradidōmi* can be
properly rendered "betray." Klassen writes:

> Not one ancient classical Greek text has so far surfaced in which
> *paradidōmi* means "betray" or has any connotation of treachery. Any
> lexicon that suggests otherwise is guilty of theologizing rather than
> assisting us to find the meaning of Greek words through usage.[7]

As such, there is no justification for a "collational notion" of treachery
and betrayal for the term. Klassen writes: "How can one 'betray

weapons' in Xenophon's *Cyro* 5.1.28? [The] meaning is clearly to 'give up, hand over, or surrender'."[8] The Greek translation of the Hebrew scriptures, known as the Septuagint (LXX),[9] also gives us no indication that *paradidōmi* can be accurately translated as "betray." It can be concluded "that the word 'to hand over' does not have a negative connection in the Greek Bible." Therefore, the answer to our original question – does the meaning of *paradidōmi* warrant two drastically different renderings within the very same sentence? – thus far is no.

Also relevant to our examination of Paul and his use of *paradidōmi* are the writings of Josephus, the first-century Jewish-Roman historian whose work is an invaluable resource to scholars of the ancient world. In a famous section of his work *The Jewish War*, Josephus relates the story of how his city of Jotapata fell to the Romans during the First Roman-Jewish War. Josephus flees the city and happens upon a cave where forty other Jews are hiding, equipped with adequate provisions. They remain in the cave until their position is given up by an unnamed woman, and the armies of Emperor Vespasian surround the cave. The group soundly rejects the soldiers' request for them to surrender in favor of a mass suicide.[10] Josephus is determined not to commit suicide and offers a prayer to God: "But, for my part, I shall never pass over to the enemy's ranks, to prove a traitor [*prodōtes*] to myself." Despite his pleas to the group to join him in surrender, they decide that it is better to die. Josephus has no choice; he must join the group. The order of death is determined by drawing lots and Josephus (he wonders if it is through the intervention of God) draws the final lot. After watching his comrades slit the throats of their neighbors one by one, only Josephus and the man he is to murder, before killing himself, remain; Josephus persuades the man to surrender with him.[11]

What Josephus does, rather than commit suicide, is hand himself and his comrade over to the Romans, a classic example of *paradidōmi*. Yet in his prayer to God his concern is not that the "handing over" will render him a traitor (*prodōtes*), but that by joining the ranks of the Romans he would be rejecting his Jewishness. The handing over and the possible charge of "traitor" are entirely separate. Josephus uses the proper Greek word *prodōtes* to communicate this, further indicating that *paradidōmi* was not understood as "betrayal." In all his writings Josephus uses the term *paradidōmi* 293 times, yet not once can it be legitimately translated as "betray"; he uses *prodōtes* ("traitor") 22 times in clear-cut examples of treachery.[12] Once again, our search for any example of "betrayal" fitting a situation in which *paradidōmi* is used has come up empty.

Let us now turn our attention to examples of *paradidōmi* in the NT.

The following definitions appear in the standard lexicon, written by Walter Bauer:[13]

1   To hand over into the custody of: a) a thing b) a person, especially of the betrayal of Jesus by Judas with accusative and dative Matt 26:15; Mk 14:10; Lk 22:4, 6; Jn 19:11.
2   Give over, commend or commit.
3   Transmit or hand over oral tradition, relate, teach.
4   Allow or permit.

Judas does not appear in the writings of Paul, yet *paradidōmi* is translated as "betray" in 1 Cor 1:23! I argue that this is a theologizing of the text, and not an accurate translation, because Judas is being read into the pericope, or passage. As a result, the first criterion is not applicable since the specific parameters are fallacious. In order for this criterion to be valid there must be adequate examples of *paradidōmi* being used to connote betrayal outside the Judas tradition. If *paradidōmi* is translated only as "betray" in regard to Judas then the rendering is invalid, for it is both special pleading and, as Klassen points out, theologizing.

The truth is, there are no examples of *paradidōmi* being translated as "betray" outside the Judas tradition. Klassen points out that "[Of] the fifty-nine occurrences of *paradidōmi* related to the death of Jesus, twenty-seven are translated 'hand over' where Judas is not mentioned and thirty-two times translated 'betray' when Judas is mentioned. The identical word!"[14] How is it that with no other examples in all of Greek literature, both classical and koine, Judas' *paradidōmi* is translated as "betray" while the same word, in different contexts, is properly rendered "handed over"? We shall seek to discover this as we unravel the subsequent layers of the Judas tradition.

READING PAUL CORRECTLY

Our examination of *paradidōmi* began as a discussion of Paul, to whom we must now return. What we can conclude from the above investigation is that had Paul, in 1 Cor 11:23, wished to convey the idea of Jesus being "betrayed," he would have used the proper form of the Greek word *prodidōmi*, the common term for conveying treachery. Had Paul wanted to intimate that Jesus had been handed over by a "traitor" he would have called the agent performing the action a *prodōtes*. Paul does neither, so 1 Cor 11:23b is properly translated "I received from the lord the same thing I gave over [*paredōka*] to you, that on the night

when he was handed over [*paradidōmi*], the Lord Jesus took bread . . ."
Any translation that renders the term "betrayed" does so without any
etymological credence.

As noted above, we have already introduced Judas into a discussion
when he has yet to be named at all. However, it was necessary for me to
do so because translators for generations have been unfaithful to the
texts. We must be careful that we do not do the same thing. Nothing
from Paul's writings gives us any indication that a Judas tradition or
even a tradition of a betrayer existed during Paul's ministry. In fact,
when one looks at 1 Cor 11:23, the earliest use of *paradidōmi* in connection with the death of Jesus, it is unclear who the agent of delivery is.
As Klassen notes, "The same verb is used by Paul in theological contexts in Rom 4:25: 'Jesus was delivered to death for our misdeeds.'
In Rom 8:23 it is God who delivers his own son and in Gal 2:20
Jesus delivers himself to death."[15] In Eph 5:2, 25, Jesus is described as
offering himself up (*paredōken*) for us and the church, respectively.
(Think of the theological ramifications if Eph 5:2 were translated "[The]
Anointed loved us and betrayed himself for us." This would not make
sense.) Who was responsible for Jesus falling into the hands of those
who crucified him? Paul offers not one answer but two, neither of
which involves Judas.

I think it is clear that Paul regarded the handing over of Jesus to
the authorities as essentially unimportant. What is central to Paul
is the events after the crucifixion. However, we can glean from Paul that
the idea of either God or Jesus being the agent of delivery was at least
theologically acceptable. In fact, if we return to *The Jewish War* and
Josephus' surrender to the Romans after the suicides of his comrades,
we see an excellent example of "handing over" being understood as an
action of God. Klassen notes that "Josephus sees God as the subject of
the 'handing over' and reminds Vespasian that God is a better general
than Vespasian, for he can deliver the Jews to the Romans without any
exertion on their part."[16] I find that Paul certainly held the same opinion as Josephus about God's act of deliverance through Jesus the
Anointed. When we examine the gospel narratives, we must ask how
and why Judas becomes the one who delivers Jesus – though not the
only one, since "God gave his only-begotten Son."

THE SYNOPTIC PROBLEM

The search for the Jesus, or in our case the Judas, of history would not
have been possible 250 years ago. We must not think that we are the

first to ask questions about the historicity of the scriptures, for surely we are not. However, certain analytical developments made possible by the important advances in independent Protestant scholarship, and the subsequent exegetical work of post-Vatican II[17] Catholics, have enabled modern scholars to investigate the scriptures in ways unthinkable two centuries ago. As I will be utilizing many of these tools in the present investigation, a brief discussion of the relevant scholarship is warranted.

Prior to the nineteenth century, scholars had been wrestling with an issue known as the Synoptic problem. For some time scholars had maintained that the similarities between the Synoptics[18] had to be attributed to one gospel pre-dating the other two, with the former being used as a template for the narrative framework of the latter. In the nineteenth century Christian Herman Weisse,[19] a German theologian and scholar, put forth a convincing solution to the Synoptic puzzle that revolutionized the field and is accepted by a majority of biblical scholars today. Weisse held that the work commonly called the Gospel According to Mark[20] was actually written before any of the other gospels, and that Matthew and Luke drew on Mark for their narrative framework. Until Weisse's declaration, popular scholarship had championed the theory that Mark was written later as a synopsis of Matthew and Luke.[21] Such a theory was unsatisfactory for reasons we do not have the space to examine here, but the argument for Markan priority is convincing for several reasons that should be discussed.

First, the Synoptics essentially follow the same narrative pattern, in both language and event; this shared material is commonly known as the triple tradition. Second, when examining the triple tradition found in the Synoptics, scholars noticed that Matthew and Luke deviate from Mark, but never in the same way or at the same time. When Matthew alters the Markan framework, Luke retains it and vice versa. Third, scholars asked: If Mark was written as a synopsis of the other narratives, why in almost every instance does the gospel contain more material than parallel passages found in Matthew and Luke? Take for example the story of the hemorrhaging woman (Mk 5:25–34//Mt 9:20–3): Mark dedicates ten verses to the tale while Matthew uses only three. Another example is the raising of Jairus' daughter (Mk 5:22–4, 35–43//Mt 9:18–19, 23–6), in which Mark uses twice as many verses as Matthew.[22] As a result, scholars concluded that Mark must be the template upon which the other two Synoptics based their narrative framework. The evidence for this theory is highly convincing, but scholars had to confront certain problems in order to maintain its integrity.

While the three Synoptics are similar in many respects, a plethora of important material found in Matthew and Luke is missing from Mark. This material includes central sayings of Jesus such as the Beatitudes, the Lord's Prayer and the golden rule. Scholars noticed that this material, shared only by Matthew and Luke (known as the double tradition), is related almost verbatim in both gospels. They also noticed that in instances where Mark mentions an event in passing, Matthew and Luke both include elaborate additions that are virtually identical.[23] Scholars asked: If Mark was used as the framework, how is it that Matthew and Luke share this material?

Above it was mentioned that great strides have been made in the past two centuries to help scholars in their search for the Jesus of history. One of the greatest contributions has been source criticism, a branch of scholarship that examines a document to discern the literary sources used to compose a particular text. Having established that Mark was the document upon which Matthew and Luke based their narrative framework, scholars hypothesized that the latter must have had access to another document containing the sayings that were common to them but missing in Mark. This document, the source critics argued, contained only the sayings of Jesus and not any elements of narration (that is, details about the actions of Jesus). They termed this hypothetical document Q, for the German word *Quelle*, meaning "source." The source critics argued that Matthew and Luke followed the narrative framework of Mark and used the Q source to fill out the discourse sections of their gospels; this is known as the Two-Document Theory.[24]

Even after one accounts for the material the Synoptics have in common and that which comes from Q, there is still material unique to Matthew and material unique to Luke that must be attributed to some other source. To explain the existence of such material, scholars hold that independent traditions were available to the individual gospel writers and that they included these traditions in their accounts. Material found only in Matthew is termed (special) M; the purely Lukan material is termed (special) L. The use of Mark, Q, M and L is known as the Four-Document Theory. I find the arguments used to support both of these theories to be highly convincing, and rely upon them for my treatment of Judas. Those who do not accept these theories are unlikely to be swayed by my later arguments.

The Q source: an overview

According to scholars' best estimations, the Sayings Gospel Q was written between 50 and 70 CE, during the same time period as the letters of Paul.[25] One may wonder why I refer to the document as a "gospel" when its salient features are so different from those of the Synoptics and John. It should be kept in mind that the gospel genre so familiar to us now was really a first-century invention. While the Gospel of Mark is the earliest canonical gospel, readers might be surprised to know that there were many other gospels not included in the New Testament. We should therefore not expect all other writings termed gospels to be identical to Mark. Gospels are literally the "good news" about Jesus, and that "good news" varied from community to community.

From the first fifty years of the Common Era come excellent examples of both the variegated natures of Christologies and the different types of writing that circulated to express these understandings. For example, the writings of Paul are properly termed epistles because that is exactly what they are, letters written to specific communities and meant to guide worship and internal affairs. As we noted in the section on Paul above, little historical or "biographical" information about Jesus of Nazareth is contained in the letters. Instead, the epistles constitute a developing theology and Christology that Paul champions over and against those of the various other Jewish Jesus-followers active at the time.

Paul is unconcerned about the historical Jesus because, for him, the truth of God's action lies outside what Jesus said and did. Instead, the truth of Jesus lies in his death and resurrection, and our subsequent salvation. Not all followers of Jesus, however, held the same view. Some communities focused on the sayings of Jesus as the most important feature of his ministry, while others felt that a proper interpretation of Jesus' life could come only from a narrative that explained his death. These are only two of the many reasons that different gospels were written.

Understanding an oral culture

It often can be hard for us in modern times to understand what it was like to live without television, radio, computers, cell phones, the Internet, mass media and widespread availability of literary resources. In the first century most people were not able to read; in fact, owning a book (then called a codex) was an expensive proposition because it had to be copied by a scribe. Texts were most often written on papyrus, which was (and still is) time-consuming to make and therefore was a valued commodity. So, instead of a culture based on the written word, our ancient counterparts relied on orality, or oral tradition. In a world where written documents were scarce and wisdom was valued, a person was most often judged on what he or she said and did.[26] This was what was remembered, what made someone notable: words and deeds. (This is also the reason there are no physical descriptions of Jesus contained in the gospels. For the most part, how one looked was not as important as what one did.)

As far as we know, Jesus wrote nothing himself, and scholars are divided on whether or not he knew how to read. Jesus gathered his disciples from the "working class" – the peasantry. While we cannot know for certain that they were all illiterate, it is highly probable that they were. Even if there was a literate person among their ranks, no one was taking notes as Jesus spoke because such was not their practice. While we should not think that everyone in the ancient world had perfect aural recall, it can be safely said that within an oral culture people are accustomed to understanding one's meaning from the spoken word.[27] So it should not come as a surprise that in the two decades after his death, many different interpretations of Jesus' words and deeds arose. These traditions are known as *kerygma*. As the *kerygma* circulated around the Roman Empire, the words that Jesus most likely spoke in Aramaic were translated into Greek, possibly Latin and a variety of other Semitic tongues. They were also elaborated upon, and made relevant to the communities in which they were preached; we can imagine that there was not uniformity in the interpretations of what Jesus said.

While we cannot stretch the comparison too far, there were certainly differences, for instance, between what Peter and James believed over and against what Paul believed. Many other centers of Christianity existed during this time, and we can comfortably infer that they had their own understanding of the *kerygma*. It seems likely that they would disagree with one another just as vociferously as Paul and Peter did. At some time an industrious person or group of people was bound to write down their community's oral tradition so as to pass it along without unnecessary or erroneous addition. Scholars argue that Q was one of these sayings collections, and that it was used by Matthew and Luke to flesh out the skeleton provided by Mark.

THE GNOMOLOGIA TRADITION

While Q is a hypothetical document reconstructed by scholars,[28] the Gospel of Thomas (more properly termed The Sayings Gospel of Thomas) is an excellent example of the tradition out of which Q emerges. A Coptic[29] rendering of Thomas was discovered near Nag Hammadi, Egypt, in 1945. Although the gospel was most likely written in Greek, scholars feel that the complete Coptic text is a good representation of the original Greek document. The collection of sayings is grouped according to theme and it contains no narrative elements. Every saying is introduced by the phrase "Jesus said . . ." or "So and so said to Jesus . . .". However, a distinct theology emerges from a reading of the document, relying solely upon the words of Jesus, not on the notion of a sacrificial death. This theology indicates to a preponderance of scholars that Thomas, like Q, belonged to a community of Jesus believers rather than to the members of a Christ cult.

Communities of believers were often founded around such documents in the Hellenistic world. Robert Miller writes:

> The students of famous philosophers, such as Epicurus or Epictetus, often collected the wise and witty sayings of their tradition into gnomologia, or "words of insight," which they might then use as they evangelized the public in the marketplaces and the streets of the ancient world. Jews and other ethnic groups of the eastern empire also gathered the aphoristic wisdom of their sages into collections of logoi sophon, or "sayings of the wise," such as one finds, for example, in the book of proverbs. The gathering of Jesus' sayings into such a collection places him among the sages of the past, the prophets of Sophia (the feminine personification of wisdom in Jewish lore) sent into every generation with her saving words of wisdom.[30]

From a Greek perspective, the formation of one's ethos was contingent upon following the words of a revered leader. Yet it must be understood that the tradition was fluid, and that the sayings contained in such a collection were not necessarily spoken by a sage or teacher. Mack writes, "Thus even a truism coined and in circulation during a later time could be culled for appropriate attribution to the collections of this or that philosopher or sage from a previous period. Founders of schools regularly got credit for the philosophies that developed in the school tradition in their name."[31] Therefore, while it was important to communities such as Q and Thomas to "know" the words of Jesus – indeed, this was the earliest way a Jesus-follower distinguished him or herself as a disciple – it was also understood that there were words attributed to Jesus that were not, in fact, uttered by him. Whereas contemporary Christians may have a problem with this, Jesus-followers in the first century did not.

Before moving on to a more detailed analysis of Q, it is important to note that scholars are certain that Thomas is not Q, for Thomas lacks some of the most important elements of Q and contains sayings not found in Matthew or Luke.[32] However, Thomas is important in understanding Q because it provides evidence that sayings gospels were written by early Jesus-followers. Scholars are divided on the date of Thomas, but many feel a first edition could have been written at the same time as Q, that is, c. 50–70 CE. I place myself firmly in this camp.

Q AND THE EARLY JESUS MOVEMENT

Although an exegesis of Q is beyond the purview of this treatment, it is important to note that scholarship is divided as to how Q should be regarded. As indicated above, some maintain that Q was merely a written collection of Jesus' sayings, which for whatever reason found its way into both the Matthean and Lukan communities and indelibly affected their gospel narratives. Others, such as Burton L. Mack, argue that the Q Gospel belonged to a community and that the document, in fact, can tell us much about the historical evolution of the Jesus movement. Mack argues that Q went through three distinct periods of formation. The first layer of tradition, Q 1, reveals a community focused on the words of Jesus. His revolutionary teachings advocate a pronounced and critical approach to living, which is analogous to philosophies of the Cynics (for a discussion of Cynic philosophy, see Chapter 4). In the second layer of the tradition, Q 2, apocalyptic images and traditional Wisdom motifs[33] are incorporated into the narrative, drastically altering the understanding of Jesus, but building upon the framework established in Q 1. The Q 3 material reflects the state of the community after the destruction of the Jerusalem Temple in 70 CE. Parallels between Q and Mark will be discussed in Chapter 3.

According to Mack, the Q 2 material is the most dynamic, for it tells us much about the evolution of the Q community. The community faced heavy persecution and was forced to establish boundaries to protect itself. Mack writes, "These sayings [Q 2 material] signal the direction in which the Q 2 people were to move as they measured loyalty to their movement . . . the question of loyalty had become an extremely important issue, and that loyalty to the movement could now be expressed in terms of loyalty to Jesus, not just in terms of keeping his words."[34] As the community came under increasing pressure, the standards of discipleship began to change. That this trend can be identified so early will be centrally important to my argument regarding the historicity of Judas Iscariot.[35]

Q is wholly unlike other gospels in that it does not contain the "proper" gospel narrative components, such as an account of Jesus' birth, miracle stories central to the other gospels, details about his death and resurrection, or even a reference to Jesus as the Anointed of God. Rather, Q depicts Jesus as a messenger of Wisdom, as Q 11:31[36] (quoted from Luke) demonstrates:

> At judgment time, the queen of the south will be brought back to life along with the members of this generation, and she will condemn them, because she came from the ends of the earth to listen to Solomon's wisdom. Yet take note: what is right here is greater than Solomon.

The "queen of the south" is the Queen of Sheba, who visits King Solomon after hearing of his fame and the grandness of Jerusalem. 1 Kings 10 states that the queen poses many difficult questions to Solomon, who in turn amazes her with his wisdom.[37] Q 11:31 presents Jesus as a figure greater in wisdom than even Solomon, a fact the Queen of Sheba will attest to herself when all are risen from the dead at "judgment time." The Q passage informs historians that: (a) the audience was most likely Jewish, or familiar with the Jewish story, for the frame of reference is a Jewish Wisdom tradition; and (b) the Truth of Jesus is to be found in his having delivered Wisdom to the Q community. One is a follower of Jesus by embodying and living this Wisdom.

The Q Gospel mentions Wisdom, either explicitly (Q 7:35//Mt 11:1, 9b; Q 11:31//Mt 12:42; Q 10:21–2//Mt 11:25–6) or implicitly (Q 11:49// Mt 23:24; Q 13:34–5//Mt 23:37–9) five times. When joined with the numerous aphoristic sayings of Jesus found throughout Q, an understanding of Jesus as a wise man strongly emerges. Clearly, Wisdom was important to the Q community and they felt it had been delivered definitively by Jesus.

Q does not present Jesus simply as the bearer of Wisdom; it also paints him as a prophet. References to Jesus as a prophet equal to or greater than the traditional prophets of Israel are found in five different pericopes: Q 6:22–3//Mt 5:11–12; Q 11:47–51//Mt 23:29–32, 34–6; Q 13:34–5//Mt 23:37–9; and Q 10:23–4//Mt 13:16–17. As Miller notes, "The people who used Q made use of a tradition according to which Israel persistently disobeyed God, rejecting God's servants, the prophets, and refusing to obey God's commandments, thereby incurring the wrath of God."[38] When one examines these passages in conjunction with those pertaining to Wisdom, an interesting under-standing of Jesus emerges: the Wisdom tradition and the prophetic tradition, hitherto unrelated, are joined together in the Q depiction of Jesus. Jesus delivers Wisdom only to be rejected, much as the prophets of Israel were rejected in their own times, with important ramifications for those who follow his teachings. Biblical scholar Richard A. Edwards writes that "In contrast [to those who reject Jesus], of course, there are those who have the insight to recognize the authority and purpose of Jesus and his followers. Their reward for following the true prophet is persecution and violence, just as the earlier prophets were persecuted."[39] The Q community itself was persecuted, but it understood this treat-ment to be an inevitable consequence of following God's prophet and deliverer of Wisdom.

What is interesting is that while Q uses the framework of the deu-teronomic historian,[40] nothing about the death of Jesus has a redemp-tive effect. Arthur Dewey observes that "The death of Jesus in the Sayings Gospel is not a focal point for the community. The words of Jesus form the atmosphere of this early community."[41] The central mes-sage of Q is that they are bearers of an important message that results only in pain, suffering and the division of families. Miller observes that "This pain can be sensed behind the vivid threats depicting how Israel will be punished for rejecting Jesus and the Q preachers 10:13–15; 11:31–2, 49–51; 13:28–9, 34–5)."[42] Indeed, the denunciations against Jesus' enemies are especially harsh and violent (Q 3:7–9; 10:13–15), reflecting a community persecuted and divided.

Understanding the Q community as it is represented in the Q Gospel provides us with an important insight into early "Christianity" and is centrally important to our investigation of Judas. Burton L. Mack writes:

> The remarkable thing about the people of Q is that they were not Christians. They did not think of Jesus as messiah or the Christ. They did not take his teachings as an indictment of Judaism. They did not regard his death as a divine, tragic, or saving event. And they did not imagine that he had been raised from the dead to rule over a transformed world. Instead they thought of him as a teacher whose teachings made it possible to live with verve in troubled times. Thus they did not gather to worship in his name, honor him as a god, or cultivate his memory through hymns, prayers, and rituals. They did not form a cult of the Christ such as the one that emerged among the Christian communities familiar to the

readers of the letters of Paul. The people of Q were Jesus people, not Christians.[43]

The Q community was dogmatically and catechistically barren, an excellent place to begin searching for evidence of Judas. Because Q is a curious document, we have a two-fold task: first, we must see if Judas is mentioned either explicitly or implicitly in Q. Second, if Judas is not found in Q, we then must see if Q sayings are changed by Matthew or Luke to refer to Judas. (I examine this latter option in Chapters 5 and 6, respectively.)

Q and Judas Iscariot

Like the letters of Paul, Q makes no explicit mention of Judas Iscariot. At first this does not seem surprising. Q is a collection of sayings, not a narrative framework. There are no mentions, in fact, of Jesus' arrest, trial and execution. The only figure contemporaneous with Jesus named specifically is John the Baptizer. Jesus' disciples are addressed as a substantive group, not as individuals.[44] The concern of Q is not historical details but a theology and understanding of Jesus that makes sense of the happenings within the community itself. However, I find it telling that Judas is entirely absent from the narrative.

As noted above, the Q Gospel makes vehement condemnations of those who supposedly opposed Jesus; though a better understanding would be that condemnations of those who oppose the Q community are placed in the mouth of Jesus, in line with the gnomologia tradition. Nevertheless, given that Q utilizes the deuteronomic framework and depicts him as a prophet rejected by his own people, why are there no sayings pertaining to the "betrayal" of Jesus by Judas? Take, for example, Q 11:49–51, quoted below.

> That is why the wisdom of God has said, "I will send them prophets and apostles, and some of them they are always going to kill and persecute. So this generation will have to answer for the blood of all the prophets that has been shed since the world was founded, from the blood of Abel to the blood of Zecheriah, who perished between the altar and the sanctuary." Yes, I tell you this generation will have to answer for it.

In this pericope, Jesus makes no mention of his own impending death. Even if we understand this passage as reflecting the theology of Q and not the words of the historical Jesus, why then is there no mention of

Judas? Even if the death of Jesus is implicit, it is given no greater weight than that of Abel and Zecheriah – according to Q the deaths of all the prophets will be accounted for. The culprits in Q are those who oppose the prophets, of which Jesus is one, yet Judas is nowhere to be seen! Why is this?

I argue that a tradition holding Judas responsible for Jesus' capture had not yet emerged. Remember, we have already established that in Paul's account of Jesus being "handed over" (*paradidōmi*), God and Jesus were understood to be the active agents. In Q there is no reference to the handing-over event, but there is a milieu in which the agents of oppression and condemnation are vehemently attacked and admonished that their actions will result in dire consequences. If the tradition of Judas depicted in Mark, Matthew and Luke–Acts was developed at the time of Q, why does Q not use it?

CONCLUSIONS

That Q and Paul do not contain the Judas material, of course, does not prove its non-existence; it does, however, raise a red flag. We must consider what Paul and Q do say about our topic. From our investigation we can determine that: (a) the Greek word *paradidōmi*, as it is used in Paul and all future gospel narratives we shall examine, is properly translated "hand over"; (b) Paul interprets the "handing over" of Jesus to have been performed by either Jesus himself or by God, an interpretation that fits soundly within his Jewish world, given Josephus' own account of God handing him over to Vespasian so as to serve a greater purpose; (c) Q is silent about the night in which Jesus is remanded into the custody of the authorities, but the gospel does contain violent polemics against enemies of Jesus, yet Judas is not mentioned anywhere; and (d) the idea that Judas has been part of the Christian story from the earliest level is unsubstantiated and should not be read into the Pauline and Q material.

We have also established that, for the communities of Q and Thomas, being a disciple of Jesus involved "knowing" the words of Jesus. Following in the Greco-Roman tradition of gnomologia, these important early documents represent two different communities that understood Jesus as a teacher/prophet, not a sacrificial lamb. We noted, albeit briefly, that there is a difference between Christ cults and Jesus believers; the former understand Jesus in terms of God's salvific action through the crucifixion and resurrection of his son, the latter through the words of Jesus. Citing the scholarship of Burton Mack, we noted that the Q community evolved its understanding of Jesus as it faced increasing persecution from the outside; I will argue in the next chapter that the Gospel of Mark also belonged to a struggling community, one that seriously questioned the authority of those who claimed to represent Jesus directly.

3   Mark: the beginning of the Judas myth

> So much romantic imagination has been lavished on the gospels for so many centuries that the modern reader does not at once see how stark they are. We automatically add novelistic details, many of which have reached people who have never entered a church or read from the Bible. Apart from the birth narratives in Matthew and Luke, where novelistic interest has already penetrated, there is not much in the rest of the gospels. This presumably means that they have been shaped precisely in order to make their point, other matter being pruned away.
>
> E.P. Sanders[1]

We often approach the Bible as though we know the gospel stories. This is especially true of those who were raised in the church. I find, however, that – when I am lecturing on the gospels or discussing a specific actor in a gospel narrative – students often attribute to one gospel details that are actually found in another. They combine the narratives, intermingling details and emerging with a picture that cannot be found anywhere in the Bible. I think this is a result of the way the Bible is approached and taught: by and large Christian sermons are based on proof texts, that is, bits and pieces of disparate writings that are treated as though they were intended to be part of a cohesive whole.

While some may regard the gospels as a unified text, from an historian's viewpoint such a practice is irresponsible and flawed. There is absolutely no historical evidence showing that the author(s) of, say, Matthew knew that one day the gospel narrative central to the Matthean community would be grouped with those of Mark, Luke and John. Therefore putting the words of Luke into the metaphorical mouth of Matthew is not sound biblical exegesis. Yet we live in a society where sound bites and the bottom line are valued more than accurate, informed knowledge of the pertinent data. Consequently, it can often be difficult for people to be cognizant of what a specific gospel has to say without imposing outside details on the narrative. We must not fall prey to such folly when discussing Judas Iscariot. We must hear what Mark has to say about Judas before we can approach Matthew and Luke–Acts; we must see how Judas changes from gospel to gospel, all the while being attentive to the details that are provided to us.

In this chapter I put forth the thesis that Judas Iscariot is an invention of the Markan community, meant to undercut the authority of "the twelve" (*tous dōdeka*). In order to prove this claim, I focus on three main themes. First, Q and Mark share material about how one is to become a follower of Jesus. Mark uses this material to systematically humiliate the twelve in the eyes of the listener/reader.[2] Second, Judas Iscariot appears in Mark's narrative three times, and each time he is introduced as "Judas Iscariot, one of the twelve." I argue that Mark does this deliberately so as to prejudice further the listener/reader. Third, in Mark's gospel, Jesus' Passion is told by using the template of the Suffering Innocent Tale. The use of this device necessitates two primary elements: the over-emphasized innocence of the Sufferer and the existence of an antagonist to oppose the protagonist. Judas Iscariot serves to fulfill both these criteria.

Q AND MARK: HOW IS ONE A FOLLOWER OF JESUS?

Mark's gospel is written in a simple style of Greek. The conjunction *kai* (and) appears an inordinate number of times, as does the word *euthos* (immediately). The gospel also uses the same phrases and constructions repeatedly, giving the overall narrative a feeling of urgency. The gospel certainly is not a polished literary masterpiece, yet it does seem to reflect the rhetorical devices of oral preaching. Scholars have for a long time debated whether or not pre-Markan units of tradition can be identified, a branch of scholarship known as form criticism. Janice Capel Anderson and Stephen D. Moore observe that form critics have sought "to classify the units of tradition of which the Gospels were thought to be composed into appropriate categories or 'forms,' such as parables, legends, myths, exhortations, proverbs, and controversy stories."[3]

Form critics have argued that by separating out these traditions and assigning them a *Sitz im Leben* ("setting in life") – that is, a function such as preaching, baptismal rite or teaching tool – one is able to understand the formation of the gospel. According to this theory, the gospel writers were not so much authors as collectors of variegated material. Martin Dibelius, an early form critic, wrote: "Only in the smallest degree are the writers of the Gospels authors; they are in the main collectors, transmitters, editors. Their activity consists in the handing on, grouping and working over the material that has come down to them."[4] Much of Mark's gospel reflects this type of collection and redaction.

For decades, scholars have contended that Mark did not have access to Q. While I agree with this conclusion, I find startling parallels between Q and Mark's criteria for how one becomes a follower of Jesus. These similarities lead me to believe that there were early oral traditions of what we might today call "standards of discipleship." I do not think we should use this terminology, however: Jesus in Q uses the term "disciples" (*mathētai*) in reference to his own followers only five times (6:20; 10:23; 12:22; 17:1; and 17:22) and only once (12:22) can it loosely be inferred that Jesus is giving them instructions regarding their mission. Conversely, in Mark's gospel, the "standards of discipleship" are to be found in conjunction with "the twelve" (*tous dōdeka*), and they are never called "the twelve disciples." Therefore, I find it more accurate to refer to "criteria for followers of Jesus" rather than "standards of discipleship."

Q contains twelve distinct instructions for followers of Jesus. For our purposes, we shall focus on only four of these right now. The first states that followers live an itinerant lifestyle (Q 9:57–62; 9:61–2; 10:3; 10:4; 10:5–6; 10:7; 10:8). The second specifies that in order to follow Jesus one must respond immediately to Jesus' call (Q 9:59–60; 9:61–2). The third instructs followers to proclaim that God's Imperial Rule is closing in (Q 10:9; 10:10–12), thus suggesting an intimate relationship between God's Imperial Rule and Jesus' ministry. The fourth states that following Jesus requires a complete dedication to the ministry, even to the detriment of one's familial obligations (Q 9:59–60; 9:61–2). I find that these four Q criteria are fulfilled implicitly in Mk 1:14–15 and Mk 1:16–20, which are quoted below (with my italics).

(14) After John was locked up, Jesus went to Galilee proclaiming God's good news. (15) His message went: "The time is up: God's *imperial rule* is closing in. Change your ways and put your trust in the good news." (16) As he was walking by the Sea of Galilee, he spotted Simon and Andrew, Simon's brother casting [their nets] into the sea—(17) since they were fishermen—and Jesus said to them: "Become my followers and I'll have you fishing for people!" (18) *And right then and there they abandoned their nets and followed him.* (19) When he had gone a little farther, he caught sight of

James, son of Zebedee, and his brother John mending their nets in the boat. (20) *Right then and there he called out to them as well, and they left their father Zebedee behind in the boat with the hired hands and accompanied him.*

In Mk 1:14–15, Jesus begins his ministry by proclaiming God's Imperial Rule. Immediately thereafter, in Mk 1:16–20, he calls Simon and Andrew, and then James and John. The passages imply that these four individuals hear Jesus proclaim that God's Imperial Rule is closing in: an implicit connection is made between hearing this proclamation and being a follower of Jesus, thus fulfilling Q criterion number three. Each of these individuals immediately joins Jesus (1:18, 20), beginning an itinerant life and thereby fulfilling Q criteria one and two. Notice that in v.20 James and John leave a family member behind, thereby fulfilling Q criterion number four. That all four selected Q criteria are met implicitly in Mk 1:14–15, 16–20 indicates to me that there were oral traditions regarding how one was to be a Jesus-follower, traditions which were known to both Q and Mark. However, to make this case, I must support my argument with more direct evidence.

How to travel

Explicit connections between Q and Mark arise when one examines the role of "the twelve" (*tous dōdeka*) in Mark's gospel.[5] After being introduced in Mk 3:13–19, the twelve disappear from the narrative until 6:7–13, which is cited below (with my italics). The Q parallels are also quoted, again with my italics.

(7) Then he summoned the twelve and started sending them out in pairs and giving them authority over unclean spirits. (8) And he instructed them not to take anything on the road, except a staff: no bread, *no knapsack, no spending money*, (9) *but to wear sandals*, and to wear no more than one shirt. (10) And he went on to say to them: "Wherever you enter someone's house, *stay there until you leave town.* (11) *And whatever place does not welcome you or listen to you, get out of there and shake the dust off your feet in witness against them.*" (12) So they set out and announced that people should turn their lives around, and they often drove out demons, (13) and they anointed many sick people with oil and *healed them.*

Q 10:4: *Carry no purse, no knapsack, no sandals.* Don't greet anyone on the road.

Q 10:9: *Cure the sick* there and tell them, "God's imperial rule is closing in."

Q 10:7: *Stay at one house*, eating and drinking what they provide, for workers deserve their wages. *Do not move from house to house.*

Q 10:10–11: (10) *But whenever you enter a town and they do not receive you, go out into the streets and say,* (11) "*Even the dust of your town that sticks to our feet, we wipe off against you.* But know this: God's imperial rule is closing in."

What is striking about Mk 6:7–13 is that it reveals the Q community and the Markan community share five *explicit* criteria regarding how one is to travel. One, followers are "sent out" (Q 10:3//Mk 6:7). Two, a follower carries no knapsack (Mk 6:8//Q 10:4). Three, a follower stays in one house until leaving the town (Mk 6:10//Q 10:7). Four, a rejected follower is admonished to shake the dust off his or her sandals as a sign (Mk 6:11//Q 10:10–11). And five, a follower is given the power to heal sick people (Mk 6:13//Q 10:9). It is also striking that Q insists that those who are sent out do not wear sandals, while Mark orders them to wear sandals; Q prohibits the carrying of a purse, and Mark the possession of spending money (Mk 6:9//Q 10:4). In addition to the four implicit connections between Q and Mark, we can now add five explicit connections and two curious parallels.

What to expect

Two more explicit similarities between Q and Mark emerge when we examine Q 14:27 and Mk 8:34, 35, cited below (with my italics).

Mk 8:34: After he called the crowd together with his disciples, he said to them, "*If any of you wants to come after me, you should deny yourself: pick up your cross, and follow me.*"

Mk 8:35: *Remember, by trying to save your own life, you're going to lose it, but by losing your life* for the sake of the good news, *you're going to save it.*

Q 14:27: *Unless you carry your own cross and come along with me— you're no disciples of mine. Whoever tries to hang onto life, will forfeit it, but whoever forfeits life will preserve it.*

These verses involve expectations of a Jesus-follower: one must take up one's own cross (Mk 8:34//Q 14:27), and one must be willing to risk one's own life in order to save it, knowing that deliberately trying to save one's life will result in its loss (Mk 8:35//Q 14:27). Considering that the Q gospel and Mark's gospel were written independently of one another, it is logical to ask how these numerous similarities can be explained.

I argue that there were early oral traditions regarding how one was to be a follower of Jesus, which began to circulate after the crucifixion. These traditions must have been well known by c.72 CE since the two unrelated communities both capitalized upon them. The ways these traditions are used by Q and Mark are telling. Where Jesus is teaching his way of life, which anyone can follow, both Q and Mark record his dicta being addressed to everyone – the crowd, disciples, apostles – without distinction. Where Jesus is giving instructions to those willing to be his missionaries, Q again records him addressing all his followers *en masse*, whereas in Mark he is speaking only to the twelve. In this regard, the Q gospel carries on the ancient gnomologia tradition: one becomes a proper follower of a leader by having knowledge of the leader's words. As such, Q does not need an individual or a group to embody the expected standards. Mark, on the other hand, places these shared criteria in terms of "the twelve" (*tous dōdeka*). Specific individuals are named and made central actors in the narrative; they are given the power to expel demons, an indication that they have the power and authority of Jesus, whom the listener/reader has encountered already as a healer and exorcist. Therefore, an important question arises: Does the Markan community understand "the twelve" as examples of how one is to follow Jesus?

Mk 8:27–30 as a test case: Peter understands Jesus

In Mk 8:27–30, Peter emerges as the only individual who understands Jesus' true identity:

> (27) Jesus and his disciples set out for the villages of Caesarea Philippi. On the road he started questioning the disciples, asking them, "What are people saying about me?" (28) In response they said to him, "[Some say, You are] 'John the Baptizer,' and others, 'Elijah,' but others, 'One of the prophets'." (29) But he continued to press them, "What about you, who do you say I am?" Peter responds to him, "You are the Anointed!" (30) And he warned them not to tell anyone about him.

While others (v.28) report that there are three major theories regarding Jesus' identity, Peter responds with certainty in v.29 that Jesus is the Anointed. The listener/reader, having been given this information in Mk 1:1, identifies Peter as having a proper understanding of Jesus and, in turn, as being a true follower. As a result, there is a positive connection between Peter and the listener/reader.

Mk 8:31–3 as a test case: Peter misunderstands Jesus

The listener/reader's positive feelings about Peter are immediately challenged in Mk 8:31–3:

> (31) He started teaching them that the son of Adam was destined to suffer a great deal, and be rejected by the elders and the ranking priests and the scholars, and be killed, and after three days rise. (32) And he would say this openly. And Peter took him aside and began to lecture (*epitiman*) him. (33) But he turned, noticed his disciples, and reprimanded (*epetimēsen*) Peter verbally: "Get out of my sight, you Satan, you, because you're not thinking in God's terms, but in human terms."

In v.31, Jesus openly predicts his own rejection, death and resurrection. In v.32, however, Peter takes exception to Jesus' predicted fate. As the passage is translated, it appears that Jesus and Peter engage in a verbal altercation. In fact, what we have in vv.32–3 is a mutual exorcism. The two Greek words given in parentheses are forms of *epitimao*, a forceful rebuke: Jesus uses this word to expel the deaf and blind demon in Mk 9:25. We have the same type of situation in vv.32–3: Peter takes Jesus aside and attempts to expel an unclean spirit from him. Jesus responds by calling Peter a Satan, or oppressor. The impact of this scene upon the listener/reader is undeniable. Peter and the twelve had been given the authority to cast out unclean spirits in 6:7, and it is reported in 6:13 that they were successful. In 8:22–3, our test case, however, Peter not only uses this ability incorrectly by trying to exorcize the very source of his power, but he himself is exorcized! The listener/reader suddenly begins to question the role of Peter. We can hear the author of Mark asking the listener/reader: Is this the type of person you want leading you?

Mk 9:14–29 as a test case: the disciples cannot expel a demon

The ability of Jesus' followers to exorcize demons is again a theme in Mk 9:14–29, quoted in part below:

> (17) Jesus asked them, "Why are you bothering to argue with them?" And one person from the crowd answered him, "Teacher, I brought my son to you, because he has a mute spirit. (18) Whenever it takes him over, it knocks him down, and he foams at the mouth and grinds his teeth and stiffens up. I asked your disciples to drive it out, but they couldn't." (19) In response he says, "You distrustful lot, how long must I associate with you? How long must I put up with you? Bring him over to me." (20a) And they brought him over to him . . . (24) Right away the father called out and said, "I do trust! Help my lack of trust." (25) When Jesus saw that the crowd was about to mob them, he rebuked the unclean spirit, and commands it, "Deaf and mute spirit, I command you, get out of him and don't ever go back inside him!" . . . (28) And when he had gone home, his disciples started questioning him privately: "Why couldn't we drive it out?" (29) He said to them, "The only thing that can drive this kind out is prayer."

In v.8, the father of the possessed child informs Jesus that the disciples have been unable to expel the demon; in v.28, the disciples themselves admit this. Note once again that only "the twelve" (*tous dōdeka*) have been given the authority to expel demons (Mk 6:7), so I find it likely that this passage is meant to indicate their failure. (Even if such is not the case, there is no clear-cut example of a disciple (*mathētēs*) being seen in a positive light in Mark; regardless of whether those who tried to drive out the demons were apostles or disciples, the message is still the same: the exorcism was a failure.)

The nature of the failure is perhaps more disturbing to the listener/ reader than the failure itself: In v.9, Jesus suggests that the inability of the disciples to cast out the demon is due to a lack of trust. This connection is made explicit in v.29, when Jesus informs the disciples that prayer is the only act that can drive out this type of demon. Certainly, the listener/reader will notice that nowhere in Mark's gospel does any disciple or member of the twelve pray. To the listener/reader, prayer seems an easy requisite for the ability to exorcize demons. Furthermore, it is the trust of the father that allows the child to be healed (v.24). The followers of Jesus cannot expel the demon because of a lack of trust; the father's trust allows the healing to be completed. Once again, we can hear Mark asking the listener/reader: Why would you trust people of this character?

MK 13: A THEMATIC CRESCENDO

Mark weaves a unique motif throughout the narrative, that of follow-ers having the ability to expel demons. This thread – not found in the earlier sources, Paul and Q – is not meant to highlight the authority of the twelve; on the contrary, it is used to undermine them. The ability to exorcize is used incorrectly by Peter in 8:31–3, when he tries to exorcize Jesus, and it is non-existent in 9:14–29, when the followers of Jesus cannot perform because of a lack of trust and the failure to pray. Mark's rejection of the twelve's claims that they can expel demons reaches a crescendo in Mk 13. Verses 3–6, 13 and 21–2 are quoted below:

> (3) And as he was sitting on the Mount of Olives across from the temple, Peter would ask him privately, as would James and John and Andrew: (4) "Tell us, when are these things going to happen, and what will be the sign to indicate when all these things are about to take place?" (5) And Jesus would say to them, "Stay alert, other-wise someone might delude you! (6) You know, many will come using my name and claim, 'I'm the one!' and they will delude many people . . . (13) And you will be universally hated because of me. Those who hold out to the end will be saved . . . (21) And then if someone says to you, 'Look, here is the Anointed,' or 'Look, there he is!' don't count on it! (22) After all, counterfeit messiahs and phony prophets will show up, and they will provide portents and miracles so as to delude, if possible, even the chosen people."

In Mk 13, Jesus, Peter, John, James and Andrew sit on the Mount of Olives across from the Temple – which Jesus has just prophesied will be knocked down to the last stone (13:2). The four men ask Jesus what will be the sign that the end is coming. Employing dramatic irony, the Markan Jesus gives detailed warnings about the coming end to the very individuals who will fail him in Gethsemane (14:33–42). However, if one regards these verses as coming from the historical Jesus, a litany of problems arise. For example, there are no historical records of Jesus believers being expelled from synagogues or being arrested c.30 CE, and many scholars argue that the historical Jesus was not an apocalyptic prophet.[6]

What Mk 13 reflects is the contemporary experience of the Markan community – which has just seen the Temple fall and has experienced a loss of members, presumably due to a lack of belief. It contains the Markan criteria for being a true follower of Jesus: People will be beaten and thrown out of synagogues (v.9); others will be arrested (v.10); still others will turn against their families (v.12); all will be hated because of Jesus (v.13a). One must understand that the time of God's Imperial Rule is coming quickly; if one cannot endure these realities, one is not a proper follower of Jesus (vv.14–20). The fear of the community is palpable in these verses; a follower is promised hardship, but, in v.13b, is also promised reward: "Those who hold out to the end will be saved!" Those who stay true to the Markan vision of Jesus shall inherit the kingdom, and only true followers receive the reward. As the listener/reader will discover by 14:72, none of the twelve holds out until the end; all of them fail dismally. (See below, "The collective failures of the twelve.")

Remember that another central question to the Markan community – in fact, to all Jesus communities in the first and second centuries – was who had authority. I argue that Mk 13:6, 21–2 are polemics against the claims to authority made by "the twelve" who presume to act in Jesus' name. The verses read: "You know, many will come using my name and claim, 'I'm the one!' and they will delude many people . . . And then if someone says to you, 'Look, here is the Anointed,' or 'Look, there he is!' don't count on it! After all, counterfeit messiahs and phony prophets will show up, and they will provide portents and miracles so as to delude, if possible, even the chosen people." To me, the message is clear: the Markan community and the listener/reader are the chosen people who are in danger of being deluded by those who claim to act in Jesus' name. To save itself from apostasy and to avoid losing the reward of salvation, the Markan community rejects the twelve (or perhaps their first generation of followers). They reject the claim that these individuals have the ability to exorcize demons, and they warn others not to be deluded. The Markan community and the listener/reader know the truth about Jesus, that he is the Anointed. Repent and await the end by staying true to Jesus, Mk 13 tells us: nothing else is necessary.

The collective failures of the twelve

Mark systematically assaults the collective character of the twelve by relating incidents in which each of Jesus' original four followers – Peter, Andrew, John and James – fails miserably. John tries to stop people from driving out demons in Jesus' name because the would-be exorcists are not members of the twelve, only to be reprimanded by Jesus (9:38–41). James and John, after Jesus issues his third prediction of the approaching sufferings, argue about who shall sit at Jesus' left and right hands during the time of glory (10:35–40). Peter, James, John and Andrew all receive specific teachings on what will be the signs of the impending end (13:3–37), only to flee in Jesus' hour of need (14:50). Indeed, Peter, John and James cannot even stay awake as Jesus awaits the arresting party (14:33–42). Peter exits the narrative in shame, denying Jesus three times, even after promising he will follow Jesus until the end, even on the peril of death (14:29, 54, 66–72). By the time the listener/reader arrives at Mk 15, the crucifixion narrative, all faith in the twelve has been lost.

Mark uses the shared Q criteria for how to follow Jesus. Mark, however, inserts this material into the narrative in a much different way. One is a follower of Jesus by knowing Jesus is the Anointed (1:1), by experiencing a change of heart (1:14), and by awaiting the return of the son of Adam (13:5–36). Unlike Q, Mark elevates specific individuals, not as exemplars, but instead as examples to the chosen people of how they might be deluded.

JUDAS ISCARIOT: A MARKAN INVENTION

Of the eight additional individuals introduced to the listener/reader in Mk 3:13–19, only one is mentioned again as an independent actor in the whole of Mark's gospel: Judas Iscariot. In 3:19, Judas is named last in the list of the twelve. Much attention has been given to the meaning of Judas' full name; ultimately, we do not know if there is significance to Judas' first name being synonymous with Judah, nor do we know the meaning of "Iscariot."[7] As discussed in Chapter 2, the Greek verb *paradidōmi* which is used to describe Judas' eventual action, is properly translated as "hand over" or "turn in," as one hands over or turns in a person or property, especially after a military conquest. Therefore, upon introduction to Judas in 3:19, the listener/reader knows only that he is part of a group, four members of which appear to understand the truth about Jesus. The listener/reader does not know if Judas' "handing over" of Jesus is a negative act, nor to whom Jesus will be handed over.

And Judas Iscariot, one of the twelve

By the time Judas reappears in Mk 14:10–11, the listener/reader no longer identifies with the twelve. As we have discovered, any claims to authority the twelve might have had have already been systematically undercut by Mark.

> (10) And Judas Iscariot, one of the twelve, went off to the ranking priests to turn him [Jesus] over to them. (11) When they heard, they were delighted, and promised to pay him in silver. And he started looking for some way to turn him in at the right moment.

The name of the twelve has been sullied. What I find curious about Judas' sudden re-emergence in Mark's narrative is that he is reintroduced specifically as "Judas Iscariot, one of the twelve." At first it may seem that such an introduction is necessary, given that it has been so long since we last heard of Judas. But I do not think the intention of Mark is so benign. Peter is first introduced in 3:16 and does not reappear until 5:37, and his membership in the twelve is not mentioned. In fact, no other member of the twelve, after 3:16–19, is identified as "one of the twelve." So why is Judas identified in this way? I argue that Mark deliberately reintroduces Judas in this manner so the listener/reader will automatically have a negative response to Judas. Notice, however, that the listener/reader responds negatively to Judas not because of the "handing over" event, but because of his association with the twelve. Judas is anathema because of the company he keeps, not the act he commits.

It is important that we do not read details into Mark's narrative. In v.10, Judas clearly approaches the ranking priests of his own volition, and seeks to turn Jesus in. However, no motive is given for this action. It is the *priests*, not Judas himself, who raise the issue of money; to claim that Judas acts out of greed is not a sustainable position. However, we also must not attempt to paint too rosy a picture: Judas seeks some way to hand Jesus over "at the right time."

The one who is dipping into the bowl with me

Mk 14:17–21, cited below, is a telling narrative: in this passage, Jesus supposedly predicts who shall hand him over.

> (17) When evening comes, he arrives with the twelve. (18) And as they reclined at the table and were eating, Jesus said, "So help me, one of you eating with me is going to hand me over!" (19) They began to fret and to say to one another, "I'm not the one, am I?" (20) But he said to them, "It's one of the twelve (*eis ek ton dodeka*), the one who is dipping into the bowl with me. (21) The son of Adam

departs just as the scriptures predict, but damn the one responsible for turning the son of Adam in! It would be better if that man had never been born!"

In v.17, Jesus arrives with the twelve; it is unclear whether other un-named individuals are present. In v.18, Jesus informs those eating with him that one of their number shall hand him over. In v.19, those present respond: they all wonder if they could be the culpable one. The listener/reader already knows this person to be Judas, so why does Mark add that the others question themselves? I answer that it is to emphasize the collective character of the twelve: none of those around Jesus has any worth. In v.20, Mark's narrative purpose becomes crys-tallized. Jesus indicates that the one who will turn him in is both "a member of the twelve" and "the one who is dipping into the bowl with me." However, Mark does not describe the dipping action. In fact, it essentially vanishes from the narrative. Notice how clumsy the passage is: there is no literary development or logical narrative progression, members of the twelve react to Jesus' proclamation in v.19, but do not react to the specifics offered in v.20. Jesus says the guilty one dips with him, but no dipping is reported. The listener/reader is left knowing only that the guilty person is Judas Iscariot, "one of the twelve." Why is this?

I argue that the answer is revealed in v.21, when Jesus declares that he must depart "just as the scriptures predict." It has been argued that Psalm 41:9 lies behind the narrative: "Even my bosom friend in whom I trusted, who ate of my bread, has lifted the heel against me." While this is a possibility, I think the key to understanding the pericope is seeing that, in Mark, there is a dramatic shift in *how* Jesus departs: someone interrupts the process – Judas Iscariot, one of the twelve. I base this conclusion on four examples from Paul's epistles, which involve Jesus being "handed over," and the thematic inconsistencies of Mk 8:31–3, 9:30–32 and 10:33–4.

As I noted in Chapter 2, Paul mentions four times the night Jesus was handed over. The first is in 1 Cor 11:23, which contains the earliest example of *paradidōmi* being used in connection with the death of Jesus, but the identity of the agent of delivery is unclear; Judas is not mentioned: "I received from the lord the same thing I gave over [*paredōka*] to you, that on the night when he was handed over [*pare-didōto*], the Lord Jesus took bread . . ." Likewise, the same verb is used by Paul in Rom 4:25: "Jesus was delivered [*paredothē*] to death for our misdeeds." Once again, Judas is not mentioned. When we read Rom 8:32, God is the agent who delivers Jesus: "He who did not withhold his own Son, but gave him up [*paredōken*] for all of us, will he not with him also give everything else he has?" In Gal 2:20, Jesus delivers himself to death: "I live by faith in the Anointed who loving me and giving himself over [*paradontos*] for me . . ." Paul, who provides us precious little historical information about Jesus, mentions Jesus being handed over four times, and never is Judas, nor any other human agent, the one responsible.

Jesus predicts his own rejection three times. The first declaration comes in Mk 8:31, when he says he will be rejected (*apodokimasthēnai*) by the elders, ranking priests and scholars. In 9:31, Jesus says he will be handed over (*paradidotai*) to his enemies (literally "men," *anthrōpōn*). In 10:33–4 there are new, more specific details: Jesus will be turned over (*paradōsousin*) to the nations (*tois ethnesin*), and "they will make fun of him, and spit on him, and flog him, and put him to death." Each time, Jesus is handed over to different agents. Even in the decades immediately following Jesus' death, there is confusion as to what exactly happened. Who was responsible? Who had a central role in Jesus being remanded to the authorities? Who were the authorities that wanted Jesus gone? The Markan community does not know, but they begin to formulate their own theory: Jesus was handed over by "one of the twelve."

In Mark's gospel Judas Iscariot is mentioned as the one who will hand Jesus over, but only in 3:19. In the three predictions made by Jesus, Judas does not appear, nor does it seem that Jesus is indicating that any human plays a role in the event. In fact, one can read the predictions with the Pauline theology in mind and there is no loss of meaning: Jesus goes to die because his death is the central event in signaling the coming of God's Imperial Rule. In Mk 14:12a, when Jesus states that he must depart "just as the scriptures predict," he is referring to God's will. There is no major theological shift.

It is only in the last third of the first century that the action of Jesus being handed over is taken away from God or Jesus himself and is placed into the hands of a specific human agent, "Judas Iscariot, one of the twelve." Judas is invented by the Markan community to humiliate the twelve and undercut their claims to authority. A narrative pattern supports this claim. Notice that, after each suffering declaration, an incident highlighting the denseness of the twelve follows. In Mk 8:32–3, Peter attempts to exorcize Jesus; in 9:33–7, members of Jesus' retinue argue about who is the greatest and who shall be number one; in 10:35–40, James and John, instead of asking Jesus what he might need in his final hours, ask Jesus to glorify them. Undeniably, the listener/reader will insert himself or herself into the narrative, knowing that a true follower of Jesus would expect to serve Jesus, not to be served by him (cf. 10:43). Simply stated, the twelve do not get it, they do not understand *who* this Jesus is.

Important questions arise: How does the denseness of the twelve lead one to conclude that Judas Iscariot does not exist? Furthermore, why would Mark invent Judas Iscariot? What could there possibly be to gain? Each of these questions must be answered if my theory is to hold.

I believe the "woe" statement of Mk 14:21 provides us with an important insight into why the Markan community might have invented Judas Iscariot. The text reads: "Damn the one responsible for turning the son of Adam in! It would have been better if that man had never been born!" For centuries Christians have read this as an indictment of Judas. I reject this reading. Rather, I find that the Markan community is making an explicit statement that the twelve (and those who follow them) attempt to interrupt the work of God. The twelve take credit for what God does, whether it be exorcisms or handing over Jesus to die. Therefore, woe to those who try to replace God. By inventing Judas Iscariot, the Markan community sends a clear message to the listener/reader: place your trust in Jesus the Anointed, not the twelve. The twelve do not know when Jesus will return, nor do they know the truth about Jesus: they reject Jesus' statements about his impending fate and, to make things worse, they attempt to insert themselves into the process.

It may seem that the "woe" statement on its own is not enough to sustain the thesis that Judas Iscariot is a fictional character meant to undercut the authority of "the twelve." The text clearly reads "damn the one [*ouai de tō anthrōpō*]" who turns the son of Adam in. The aspersion is cast upon an individual, not a group of people. Therefore, the question still holds: how does the guilt of Judas Iscariot sully the twelve as a whole?

MK 14:27–42: THE "ROCK" NO MORE

To answer the question about Judas Iscariot, we must look at Simon Peter. Simply stated, the Markan community does not like Simon Peter. Such a statement may seem harsh; many may bristle at its supposed arrogance. However, when one reads Mark's gospel, it becomes clear that no one around Jesus fails quite so dismally as Simon Peter. For thousands of years, Christians have theologized Peter's denial of Jesus, claiming that he is an archetype for faith; one can fail, it is believed, but one can be redeemed.

Nevertheless, exegetes rarely turn to Mark's gospel for proof texts supporting this claim. In Mark, Peter is not redeemed: the Markan Peter does not receive the keys to the kingdom as he does in Matthew (16:17–19); the Markan Peter does not see the Risen One, as he does in Luke–Acts (24:34; 24:36–53). In Mark, Peter promises he will stay by Jesus until the end, but he does not. In fact, in Mk 14:27–42, the rejection of the twelve as a substantive group is made clear:

> (27) And Jesus says to them, "You will all lose faith. Remember, scripture says, "I will strike the shepherd and the sheep will be scattered! (28) But after I'm raised I'll go ahead of you to Galilee." (29) Peter said to him, "Even if everyone else loses faith, I won't!" (30) And Jesus says to him, "So help me, tonight before the rooster crows twice, you will disown me three times!" (31) But he repeated it with more bluster: "If they condemn me to die with you, I will never disown you!" And they took the same oath—all of them . . . (33) And he takes Peter and James and John along with him, and he grew apprehensive and full of anguish. He says to them, "I'm so sad I could die. You stay here and be alert!" . . . (37) And he returns and finds them all sleeping, and he says to Peter, "Simon, are you sleeping? Couldn't you stay awake for one hour? (38) Be alert and pray that you won't be put to the test! Though the spirit is willing, the flesh is weak."

Several details should command our attention. One, Jesus tells them that all the members of the twelve will lose faith. In this way, 14:27 parallels 14:19; none of those around Jesus has any worth. Two, there are objections to Jesus' bold statements, once again mirroring the Passover narrative. This time, however, it is Peter, with whom the listener/reader once identified, who declares in v.29: "Even if everyone loses faith, I won't!" In v.30, Jesus informs Peter that before the rooster crows twice that very night, Peter will have denied him thrice. Peter once again declares his intention of staying true to Jesus (v.31). Peter is given one last chance to prove his dedication to Jesus; the listener/reader waits with bated breath. Three, notice that all the members of the twelve (literally "and also all said" – *de kai pantes elegon*) make the same oath (v.31) as Peter. Mark has not told us that Judas left; we can only assume that Judas is present and makes the oath, and Jesus allows it. This is significant because, through the shared oath, Mark connects the twelve to one another in word and deed: Peter's oath is Judas' oath. All subsequent actions made by individual members of the twelve will reflect upon the group as a whole. In the ancient world, in which the dyadic[8] personality affected every individual, this deliberate connection would not have been lost on the Markan community. United by an oath, the twelve no longer act as individuals but as a collective; they share in guilt and success.

In Mk 14:33, Jesus takes Peter, James and John along with him and confesses that he is full of anguish. He asks them to stay awake and alert. Notice that he does not ask them to pray with him, nor do they offer to accompany him. Even in the hour of his greatest need, the twelve are incapable of praying with Jesus. Until the end, they lack trust, even though they have just pledged trust and allegiance. Jesus is in agony as he prays alone in Gethsemane; the listener/reader prays with Jesus while the twelve sleep. Indeed, in v.37, he discovers that his chosen ones are unable to stay awake for even an hour. This proves to be too much for Jesus. In v.37, Jesus directly addresses Peter for the final time in Mark's gospel and he calls him Simon! This is a powerful moment. According to the Markan community, Peter is not the foundation of the church. Even if Simon was the "rock," says Mark, Jesus took it back when he realized Peter was weak. To cap it all off, Jesus hopes Simon Peter will not be tested for he will surely fail. This, of course, proves true in Mk 14:54, 66–72. Peter does not repent of his actions; he breaks down and starts to cry. He disappears from the narrative entirely. The sarcasm of the Markan narrator is almost palpable: this is the "rock"?

THE ARREST

In Mk 14:43–5, quoted below, the oft-mentioned "handing over" of Jesus occurs:

> (43) And right away, while he was still speaking, Judas, one of the twelve, shows up, and with him a crowd, dispatched by the ranking priests and the scholars and the elders, wielding swords and clubs. (44) Now the one who was to turn him in had arranged a signal with them, saying, "The one I'm going to kiss is the one you want. Arrest him and escort him safely away!" (45) And right away he arrives, comes up to him, and says, "Rabbi," and kissed him.[9]

Once again, Mark emphasizes that it is "Judas Iscariot, one of the twelve" who performs the action. This addendum is significant: three of the other members of the twelve – Simon, John and James – have been unable to stay awake with Jesus. In a few short verses, Peter will deny Jesus; so too, in vv.43–5, another member of the twelve, Judas, fails Jesus. Mark goes to great lengths to ensure that the listener/reader knows with whom Judas is associated.

Another significant detail is revealed in the arrest of Jesus. The arresting party is comprised of the ranking priests, scholars and elders; there is no doubt that Mark places responsibility for the death of Jesus upon those who plot against him, which includes certain members of the Jewish hierarchy. However, he also places responsibility upon "the twelve." The oath of fealty, uttered a short time before, is forgotten by the twelve who, it is reported in Mk 14:50, "all deserted him and ran away." According to Mark, it is not only the Jewish elite who play a role in Jesus' death, but also those who claim to be the foundation of the early Church. Mark is an even-handed castigator: reject the Jews who rejected Jesus, and reject the Jesus-believers who rejected Jesus. The listener/reader knows that true followers stay true until the end (cf. 13:13b); none of the twelve meets this criterion.

The Suffering Innocent Tale

It is bold, and perhaps presumptuous, to state that Judas Iscariot never existed. Many may not be swayed by my arguments and, certainly, valid objections can be raised. However, the strongest evidence that Judas Iscariot never existed emerges when one looks at the Passion narrative in Mark's gospel, where we find not an historical record of Jesus' death, but rather a story that is fleshed out using the primary components of the Tale of the Innocent Sufferer (also known as the Tale of the Vindicated Sufferer).

Arthur J. Dewey, the biblical scholar – in his article "Can we let Jesus die?" – argues that the original Passion narrative can be found embedded in the Gospel of Peter.[10] Calling the Passion material P, Dewey holds that the community that formed P uses Hebrew Bible biblical passages and places them within the framework of the Hellenistic Tale of the Vindicated Sufferer. According to Dewey, the communities of Mark, Matthew, Luke–Acts and John follow suit. Dewey writes:

> The Tale of the Vindicated Sufferer forms the template for all of the passion stories. In this Tale the actions and claims of an innocent person provoke his opponents to conspire against him. This leads to an accusation, trial, condemnation, and ordeal. In some instances this results in a shameful death. The hero of the story reacts characteristically, expressing his innocence, frustration, or

trust in prayer, while there are also various reactions to his fate by characters in the tale. Either at the brink of death or in death itself the innocent one is rescued and vindicated. This vindication entails the exaltation and acclamation of the hero as well as the reaction and punishment of his opponents.[11]

What is significant is that P, unlike the later Passion narratives, does not assign blame to the ranking priests or any other individual for the death of Jesus. Dewey writes, "Rather, the 'people' are responsible for the death of Jesus ... the 'people' are sinful, yet able to repent."[12] In P, there is collective guilt, but also the possibility for collective forgiveness: Jesus dies as a savior of humanity, which includes both Jew and Gentile. The death of Jesus in P is more inclusive, benefiting all.

Dewey argues that Mark also employs the skeletal structure of the Suffering Innocent Tale to make sense of the death of Jesus. Mark's use of the Tale, however, is very different from that in P. Writing after the fall of Jerusalem, Mark must make sense of the turbulent and violent world in which the community is living. Undoubtedly, the Markan community has faced persecution (cf. Mk 13) and they have lost members who were once on the "inside" (cf. Mk 4). Dewey writes:

> Now the Tale is retold tying the fate of Jesus to that of his people. He dies a martyr's death on behalf of "many" (14:24). As the story is more finely drawn, lines of loyalty are indicated. Blame begins to take on human features. The leaders of the people figure greatly in the tragic events. We have gone beyond the general critique of the "people" in Peter. The Markan version of the Tale becomes another way of defining the followers of Jesus. In brief, the death story of Jesus was not told to bring the community back to the actual events. Rather, the story is told to make sense of the persecution and deaths experienced by those in the Markan community. They saw that, just as their leader was given up to the demonic powers and was vindicated, they too were to endure tribulation in order to look with hope to their imminent vindication.[13]

With such a reading of Mark's gospel, it becomes clear that a proper follower of Jesus stays true until the end (13:13b) and accepts the "cup" (a symbol for martyrdom; see 10:38; 14:36) given to them, even if it results in death. The listener/reader in Mark's community, having faced heavy persecution, would reject with prejudice figures such as Peter, Andrew, James and John, all of whom fail to stay true to Jesus.

None of the aforementioned figures embodies any of the characteristics expected of a proper follower of Jesus. Why would the Markan community have any use for them?

What also becomes clear when one reads the Passion narrative as a deliberate retelling of the Suffering Innocent Tale is that, since blame for the death of Jesus is assigned to those on the outside, Judas Iscariot becomes a necessary element in the story. For Jesus to be the Innocent One who is Vindicated, he must face adversity; for Jesus to be the perfect protagonist, he must have an antagonist. Who better than a boon companion? An intimate relationship (usually that of brothers) between the martyr and the persecutor is common in ancient mythology: Osiris and Set, Romulus and Remus, Baal and Mot, Cain and Abel.[14] By creating Judas Iscariot and giving him a central role in the Tale of the Innocent Sufferer, Mark is able to blame Jesus' death on both the Jewish leaders with whom Judas acts in collusion and on the twelve who claim to minister in Jesus' name.[15]

CONCLUSIONS

After the crucifixion, a central issue was how one was to be a follower of Jesus. Oral traditions containing specific criteria began to circulate in the years immediately following Jesus' death and were well known, by my conservative estimate, by no later than c.72 CE. Although I find an earlier date more likely, it is difficult to substantiate. We can find these oral traditions embedded in both Q and Mark, but the two gospel communities use the material very differently. For the Q community, one is a follower of Jesus by knowing his words, an excellent example of an ancient gnomologia community. No specific individuals are presented as examples of how one is to be a true follower of Jesus. The Markan community, on the other hand, does elevate specific individuals, not as examples *par excellence*, but as epitomes of failure. The shared material on how to be a follower of Jesus is used exclusively in conjunction with the twelve, who are systematically discredited and humiliated in Mark's gospel. For Mark, one is a follower of Jesus by holding out until the end, even if it requires dying a martyr's death, like the Anointed.

The figure of Judas Iscariot is not found anywhere in Christian writings prior to 72 CE, whereas half a dozen other disciples are named in earlier sources such as Paul. Not mentioned in Q, P or the epistles of Paul, Judas suddenly appears upon the scene forty years after the death of Jesus. It is highly telling that Judas emerges in Mark's gospel. Mark, who clearly despises the twelve and does not recognize their authority, makes a concerted effort to link Judas with the twelve by using the addendum "one of the twelve" every time Judas appears in the narrative. This is not done in reference to any other member of the twelve. Mark also uses the Hellenistic Tale of the Innocent Sufferer to make sense of Jesus' death; unlike P, which also uses this template, the blame for Jesus' death is assigned to specific individuals who are not given the opportunity to repent: the Jewish hierarchy and the twelve. Judas Iscariot, as a boon companion of Jesus, is fabricated to highlight the untrustworthy nature of the twelve and also to fulfill a necessary requirement of the Tale, that of an antagonist whose perfidy highlights the innocence of the Sufferer.

Part II
Death

4   Whether 'tis nobler

There is but one truly serious philosophical problem, and that is
suicide.

Albert Camus[1]

No one ever lacks a good reason for suicide.

Cesare Pavese[2]

In June of 2002, four months before Stephen's body was found floating
in the Ohio River, I was finishing my BA degree at Antioch University
McGregor in Yellow Springs, Ohio. I had already walked in the gradu-
ation ceremony a month before I had officially completed my coursework, rendering the whole experience rather anticlimactic. The final
quarter, as often is the case for undergraduate students, was harried:
I had to meet deadlines for my senior project, finish coursework for
two classes, and make preliminary preparations to begin the master's
program at Xavier University. In a way, I thought little about what was
going on around me, for I was so focused on finishing a degree I had
begun eight years and three schools earlier that any concerns not directly related to my immediate goal became secondary. I provide this
information as background because, at the time, I was unaware of
how important a seemingly trivial comment made by a classmate later
would become.

In the summer of 2003 I signed up for a Modern World Literature
course at Antioch. I have always been an avid reader, but I reasoned
that pursuing a graduate degree in theology would leave me little time
to read literature unrelated to my chosen field. The prospect of focusing on theology as a specialized discipline excited me, but, in a manner
of speaking, it also seemed esoteric considered my academic training to
date. Both my parents are highly educated people: my father holds a
PhD in English literature and has been a professor for most of my life.

My mother, who holds a master's degree in English literature, has completed coursework for a doctorate, and has been both an adjunct professor and a professional editor for over two decades. While growing up, books were always being thrust into my hands.

By the time I was fifteen, I had read a good deal of the works by the Harlem Renaissance writers, understood the significance of magical realism in contemporary literature and could present a cogent thesis on why the books commonly read in high school are an inadequate representation of world literature. What I appreciated about reading, even from a young age, was the insight it provided me into life outside my dull Ohio town. I assumed that everyone loved to read as much as I did and for the same reasons. I felt – and still do feel – that literature's greatest power lies in its ability to transform one's worldview and force one to critically analyse cultural assumptions. Unfortunately, I have found that not everyone shares this opinion.

THE ANSWERS ARE OBVIOUS

In the Modern World Literature course I read a variety of short stories by such noted authors as Albert Camus, Jorge Luis Borges and Gabriel García Márquez; but it was a story by Yukio Mishima, entitled "Patriotism," that would provide the context for the discussion that affected me so deeply months later. Mishima is perhaps best known for his novel, *The Sailor Who Fell From Grace with the Sea*, and his modern Noh plays, but he was also a man of deep personal convictions. Fiercely loyal to his country, Mishima ended his own life by committing *seppuku* – ritual suicide by disembowelment – when the Japanese emperor lost his imperial power in 1970. Mishima's belief in the mystical power of Japanese militarism, in which the soldier is inextricably connected spiritually to the country and its leader, is expressed in "Patriotism."

The story takes place in Japan during the winter of 1936. The discovery of the bodies of Lieutenant Shinji Takeyama and his young wife Reiko is related to the reader in a perfunctory manner:

> On the 28th of February, 1936 (on the third day, that is, of the February 26 Incident), Lieutenant Shinji Takeyama of the Kono Transport Battalion—profoundly disturbed by the knowledge that his closest colleagues had been with the mutineers from the beginning, and indignant at the imminent prospect of Imperial troops attacking Imperial troops—took his officer's sword and

ceremonially disemboweled himself in the eight-mat room of his private residence ... His wife, Reiko, followed him, stabbing herself to death. The lieutenant's farewell note consisted of one sentence: "Long live the Imperial Forces." His wife's, after apologies for her unfilial conduct in thus preceding her parents to the grave, concluded: "The day which, for a soldier's wife, had to come, has come ..." The last moments of this heroic and dedicated couple were such as to make the gods themselves weep. The lieutenant's age, it should be noted, was thirty-one, his wife's twenty-three; and it was not half a year since the celebration of their marriage.[3]

As the story unfolds, the reader cannot help but be moved by the elegance of Mishima's prose. Through the use of analepsis and prolepsis, the author relates the final hours of the couple's life. The narrative vacillates between morbid eroticism – the couple's impending suicide and their final act of making love are described in equally sensuous language – and mystical militarism.

Yet this account of the conventions of honor revered in Eastern cultures goes against a Western reader's sensibilities, giving the story a force and effect not usually found in contemporary literature. The couple performs detailed preparations for the final act of *seppuku* with great attention to aesthetics and ethical propriety, and anyone who is unfamiliar with Japanese society will no doubt be left with feelings of unease and discomfort. However, it seemed to me impossible not to be affected, in one way or another, by the powerful narrative. I was looking forward to the classroom discussion, recalling the spirited and enlightened conversation about China that followed a reading of Li Po's poetry and Shen Fu's *Six Records of a Floating Life* in a different course. I hoped an insightful discussion about pre-World War II Japan, as presented in Mishima's story, would result.

My fellow students indeed were affected by the story, yet few seemed willing to discuss the cultural significance of the narrative. While most were disturbed by the latent and overt sexuality and its connection to death, what seemed unacceptable to one woman in particular was the fact that the couple committed suicide as a form of protest. Nothing, she assured us, could ever cause her to kill herself. As the discussion burgeoned into various conversations, I quietly queried the woman, a self-confessed Christian who belonged to a non-denominational church, about why she found suicide so repugnant. Without hesitation she replied: "Because people who kill themselves go to hell."

That was it, cut and dried: take your life and commit your soul to the fires of hell for eternity. At the time I found her response slightly amusing, if only because she would not allow for any exceptions. There was no room for a discussion of differing cultural mores. She completely dismissed the fact that suicide is regarded by many cultures as a noble way to meet death. I informed her that in certain nomadic communities elderly patriarchs and matriarchs, after receiving the proper signs from the gods, say goodbye to their families and wander out into hostile environs, settle down next to a tree and await death, in whatever form it may come. Or that in other cultures, such as Scythian society, those who are feeble, ill or advanced in years, burn themselves alive so as to prevent their loved ones from having to kill them or watch them die of disease. In fact, in these societies, awaiting a natural death was considered dishonorable as one was defeated by death instead of conquering it with one's own hand.

Is this act of suicide, I asked my fellow student, though done so as not to tax the community or reduce the amount of food available to the younger generations, one that will send the suicide to hell? Yes, she said, the Bible says that the act of suicide is an affront to God. Answers seemed so easy for this woman; she was certain in her knowledge of life and death, and she had the signature of God to back up her claims. Yet her confidence belied an unwillingness to think critically; she offered no specific scriptural citations to support her opinion, nor was she willing to engage in a discussion about the legitimacy of differing cultural mores. Her response was born more out of emotion than intellectual credence. I also imagined that she had never had a family member commit suicide.

A few hours later, discussing the conversation with a close friend and fellow student over a few beers, I came up with other possibilities I wanted to put before my classmate. What of the people in the World Trade Center Towers who, during the tragic attacks of 11 September 2001, jumped to their deaths rather than die of smoke inhalation? Are they in hell? If so, why? How were their actions an affront to God? If not, where is the line drawn between acceptable and unacceptable suicide? Where do these distinctions come from? Philosophy? Scripture? Cultural mores? Furthermore, I wondered, how do we as a culture define suicide? Is it simply the act of taking one's own life with one's own hands? If so, how do we explain physician-assisted suicide? Must we also include in our definition of suicide the act of placing oneself in a situation where death is the inevitable and desired result? If so, how does this understanding of suicide differ from martyrdom?

Did the Christians who defied Nero's edicts in the second century not purposely place themselves in a position where death was the only possible result? Did they not regard death as a better option than living in a world incompatible with their beliefs? In doing so, did they not commit suicide? Perhaps an even more basic and difficult question is: Did the historical Jesus commit suicide if he was aware of his own impending doom? While I maintain that it is questionable whether the Jesus of history prognosticated his own death, the fact that Christians believe he did must be addressed. By continuing in his subversive activity and forcing the hand of the Roman Empire, was Jesus a martyr or a fool? Undoubtedly there is a fine line between martyrdom and suicide, a line blurred by cultural beliefs and religious sensibilities, but the subtle distinctions between the two are fraught with theological difficulties that one must attempt to reconcile.

As I mentioned in the prologue, suicide has long been a familiar, if not complicated, issue for me, dating back to junior high school. Facing such a stark subject at a young age has provided me with a unique perspective. I understand what it is like to feel strongly about an issue, yet be unable to support an opinion with little more than emotional polemic, much like my fellow classmate at Antioch. But rooting one's opinion in emotion alone does not foster meaningful dialogue, a fact I became all too aware of during my high-school years.

When I was a senior in high school, one year after I had written and performed the one-act play in which I cryptically beseeched my father to discuss his brother's suicide with me, I was cast in the musical *Jesus Christ Superstar* by Andrew Lloyd Webber and Timothy Rice. One afternoon, close to opening night, I was in a classroom with a teacher for whom I was a teaching assistant. This teacher was originally from Louisiana and had been, if memory serves, a lifelong Catholic. Her sons were in Catholic high school and were looking at going to Catholic universities; she, rightfully so, was very proud of her faith. Although I was a self-professed atheist at the time, this did not prevent us from getting along quite well. She was more than a teacher to me: she was one of my earliest mentors.

On that spring day in 1994 when I was preparing for my role as Pontius Pilate, she and I got into a discussion about Judas Iscariot. She informed me that she liked the musical, but had problems with how positively Judas was portrayed. With my confidence bolstered by the little bit of reading I had done as research for the play, I asked her how Jesus could have completed his "destiny" if Judas had not handed him over to the authorities. Furthermore, I continued, how could Judas be in hell if he had done what needed to be done in order to fulfill God's plan? She looked at me benignly and replied, "Judas' sin was not his betrayal of Christ, Aaron. It was the fact that he committed suicide.

He did not trust God. He took control away from God and put it into his own hands. That is the greatest sin one can commit."

I was dumbstruck by her response, not because I thought she was wrong – for at the time my knowledge of the Bible was vapid, at best; rather, I did not know how to continue the conversation. The foundation of my argument was undercut by this displacement of sin: could there be any redeeming quality to Judas' act if he committed the greatest sin of all, that of denying God? Although I could not put it in these terms at the time, I wondered if Judas violated the very foundation of Jewish faith, voiced through the Shema, by killing himself. Did he not love God with all his heart and all his soul because he hung himself after seeing Jesus beaten and bloodied? I could not provide answers to these questions by simply saying that I was right because I felt strongly about it.

My personal, emotional and intellectual journey around the question of suicide really began in the spring of 1994 with that conversation. Only a few weeks later, in another classroom discussion involving some fellow classmates and a student teacher named Mr Jackson, I was nearly removed from the class for becoming so enraged that I lost my composure and called Mr Jackson an "ignorant fool." As I recall, the conversation began after a student read aloud a newspaper article about Dr Jack Kevorkian, a Michigan-based physician who had invented a suicide-machine that enabled terminally ill patients to end their lives voluntarily. Several people had used Dr Kevorkian's machine, under his supervision, and had successfully ended their lives peacefully and painlessly. Mr Jackson immediately said that Dr Kevorkian should be thrown in prison for murder. I passionately disagreed: what of the individual's right to determine his or her own end? Is it not implicit in our Bill of Rights that living freely means dying freely as well? No, Mr Jackson replied. No one person has the right to kill themselves; it constitutes a crime against the state. How is it, I asked, that the federal government could send young men off to die in Southeast Asia for a war we started, yet a woman who is suffering a slow, painful death from ovarian cancer cannot end her agony and prevent her family from watching her undignified demise?

Mr Jackson replied that it is the responsibility of the family to comfort the afflicted person until nature finishes its course, whereas it is the duty of the government to protect its interests, even if that involves sacrificing the lives of its citizenry. No civilized society, the future history teacher informed me, has ever advocated suicide. To do so would undermine the effectiveness of the government. Furthermore, he assured me, suicide is for the weak, for those who want only to experience the good in life but are unable to accept that often we are subject to seemingly intolerable pain. Indeed, suicide is the ultimate act of betrayal because it leaves others to clean up your mess. Deeply angered by this statement, I informed Mr Jackson that my uncle had killed himself. Was Fred, I inquired, therefore a weak man who had no regard for his family? Mr Jackson was silent for a moment, obviously weighing his words, and then responded: Yes. It was then that I hurled the invective against him.

At the time I, like most teenagers, did not have the wherewithal to divorce myself from my emotions and engage in a purely intellectual discussion, nor did I have a knowledge of the relevant facts to construct an intricate, well-reasoned argument favoring one's right to die. Leaving my hometown, however, and attending college in Kalamazoo, Michigan, opened up a whole new world to me. Exposed to ideas and subjects I was hitherto ignorant of, I began an intellectual journey that allowed me to suppress my natural desire to defend a personal conviction with emotion alone, in favor of a well-composed thesis supported by informed, relevant points. As my aptitude increased, physician-assisted suicide in particular, and euthanasia in general, became one of my academic focuses.

In my third year of university studies I attended Trinity College in Dublin, Ireland, for one year. In the first term I took an ethics course in which I was required to do a lengthy presentation on a contemporary ethical issue: I chose euthanasia, and did extensive research on the case of Katherine Quinlan, a young American woman who had been kept alive by life-support machines for over a decade. Her family wanted to "pull the plug," but as Ms Quinlan had no living will, there was opposition from the hospital and the state. I was in favor of the family's right to remove her from the life-support machines, but I was required to root my position in sound theory. I read a number of ethicists' views on the topic and was introduced to issues such as quality of life versus quantity of life, how various cultures have typically defined autonomy and bodily integrity, and what criteria are used by medical science to determine what constitutes "life." Not surprisingly, I found that there is no consensus on any of these issues, medically or philosophically. Some physicians maintain that a doctor's duty is to preserve life at any cost, while others hold that a physician must evaluate the quality of life the patient can expect before taking extraordinary measures. Ethicists are just as divided: some hold that suicide goes against natural reason, while others maintain that nothing is more intrinsically reasonable.

In the search for solid answers, I turned my attention to the ancient Greeks and Romans, whose ideas, for better or worse, the West has inherited. In the remaining pages of this chapter, I give a broad overview of the various attitudes toward suicide in both the ancient world and European culture. Particular attention is paid to the Greek philosophers and what the Hebrew Bible has to say about suicide.

Problems with the term "suicide"

To this point, I have used the term "suicide," primarily because it is the accepted term, and it can be readily understood by the reader. Yet "suicide" is a very curious word. In fact, it is relatively modern and did not enter the English vernacular until the seventeenth century. In all the languages of the ancient world, there is not a single word analogous to "suicide" that can be found. "Suicide" supposedly derives from the two Latin words for "self" and "killing." However, there is no Latin word *suicidum*, and according to the rules of Latin word building, "suicide" actually translates to "the killing of a pig."[4] There is no word in ancient or koine Greek for suicide; rather, there are expressions that describe the action of taking one's own life: "to grasp death" (*lambano thanaton*), "to end life" (*teleutao bion*), "to die voluntarily" (*hekousios apothneisko*), "to remove oneself from life" (*exagein heauton tou biou*), "to kill oneself" (*kteinein heauton*) and "to destroy oneself" (*diaphtheirein heauton*).[5] Adjectival descriptions for one who performed the act of self-homicide were even more idiosyncratic: *authocheir*, meaning "own-handed," or, in the late first century CE, *autothanatos*, literally meaning "dying through oneself."[6]

Suicide has become a pejorative term in our society, although it seems that historically the word evolved to remove the notion of murder from self-inflicted death.[7] Given that it has no real etymological basis and that it traditionally has been accompanied by attitudes of disdain, even abhorrence, I prefer, like many other historians, to use the phrase "voluntary death." Perhaps this is no better, and even an unnecessary deviation, but, in my opinion, it better connotes what we are talking about, the volitional act of ending one's own life.

VOLUNTARY DEATH IN THE ANCIENT WORLD

In any kind of slavery the way lies open to freedom. If the soul is sick and because of its own imperfection unhappy, a man may end its sorrows and at the same time himself . . . In whatever direction you turn your eyes, there lies the means to end your woes. Do you see that cliff? Down there is the way to freedom. Do you see that ocean, that river, that well? There sits freedom at the bottom. Do you see that tree . . . ? From its branches hangs freedom. Do you see that throat of yours, that stomach, that heart? There are ways to escape from slavery. Do you ask what is the path to freedom? Any vein in your body![8]

When the first-century philosopher Seneca wrote the words quoted above, he lived in a world where people were beginning to accept that the individual had the right to decide when and how to end his or her life. In many ways, this was a revolutionary development. I say this not out of a desire to defend my own brother's death, but out of an appreciation for the evolution of history. During Seneca's era, and for centuries preceding it, the predominant social theory held that a person's body and life belonged to the state, not to the individual agent. To end one's own life was an act of treason. From the ancient Greeks had been inherited the idea that a person was required to seek permission from the government in order to kill themselves. Compelling evidence had to be given, most often involving how one's life would be a detriment to society and how one's death would be an asset. The final decision rested not with the individual, but with the state.

Perhaps the most famous self-inflicted death in the ancient world was that of Socrates, who chose to drink hemlock rather than face exile. Socrates felt that it was not proper to kill oneself unless one had received a divine sign (*anangke*). *Anangke* may be loosely translated as "necessity" or "compulsion." According to Socrates, this sign could come only from the gods. Indeed, the entire philosophical debate regarding voluntary death in the Greco-Roman world seems to have revolved around how one discerns the *anangke*. From Plato to Cicero, Cato to Plotinus, the great thinkers of the ancient world commented on the issue of voluntary death.[9] While an exhaustive account of these various theories is both unnecessary and impossible, a brief summary will go a long way to serve our purpose of looking at the death of Judas Iscariot in Mt 27.

The only group that absolutely forbade meeting death through one's own hand was the Pythagoreans. They believed that being embodied is a punishment, that the body is actually a prison cell. By ending life through an act of volition was, in a sense, an attempt to escape from prison. The gods would not look kindly upon this, for only they could separate the body and the soul, which were inextricably linked. Voluntary death was an affront to the gods, for it took control away from the divine.[10] Therefore, voluntary death was unacceptable in any situation.

All philosophical groups in the ancient world allowed voluntary death, to greater or lesser degrees, provided a person received the proper *anangke*. How one received this sign was ambiguous. For example, the philosopher Plato, in his *Laws*, states that the *anangke* most often must come from the *polis* or community. Exceptions could be made in the case of devastating misfortune or intolerable social shame.[11] Therefore, the *anagke* was received because of a loss of honor; one could, to varying degrees, restore honor through self-inflicted death. The Cynics, on the other hand, felt that a person could be compelled to leave this world if one could not continue the proper type of life, that is, a life that conformed with the principles of Cynicism. Many Cynics killed themselves because of old age; therefore, the *anangke* could be recognized when a person could no longer live a free, self-sustaining existence. One killed oneself so as not to lose honor, not because honor had already been lost. No permission from the state was needed, for the Cynics believed in complete freedom, particularly from the government.

For the philosophical schools that allowed voluntary death, the primary consideration was that the decision be rational. The Stoics and Epicureans, who held different ideas about attaining *eudaimonia*, or the good life, both maintained that the decision to take one's own life could be done rationally (*eulogos*). While they held that one should endure until the end of life, both schools believed that it is sometimes more wise to die than to live. The Stoic philosopher Chrysippus, for example, claimed that voluntary death is an appropriate act (*kathekon*) when one can no longer live in accordance with nature.[12] Epicurus, the founder of the Epicureans, beseeched his followers to decide if they wanted death to come to them, or if they should go to death. A person could rationally decide that a truly happy life could no longer be realized, and that voluntary death was the logical remedy.

Seneca, also a Stoic and a contemporary of Jesus, felt that in certain situations Fate compelled humans to kill themselves so as to attain freedom. He writes in *On Providence*:

> Above all, I [Providence] have taken pains that nothing should keep you here against your will. The way is open. If you do not choose to fight, you may run away. Therefore, of all things I have deemed necessary for you, I have made nothing easier than dying. I have set life on a downward slope; if it is prolonged only observe and you will see what a short and easy path leads to freedom.[13]

For the Stoics, the concern was not with one taking his or her own life, but that it be done correctly by "seizing the right moment" as defined by the divine Logos. The individual logos could act in concord with the divine Logos and commit self-homicide; the individual, however, had to be certain that the signs were being read correctly.[14] The problem always is, that once one is dead, the decision to die cannot be defended. Indeed, the death is judged either rational or irrational by those left behind.

Historically, the philosophical school that had the most influence during the time of Jesus was Neoplatonism. Plotinus, the founder of the school, argued against the Stoic and Epicurean position that voluntary death could be rational. In this way, the Neoplatonists were more like Pythagoreans than traditional Platonists. Plotinus nevertheless was supremely concerned with the soul and he felt that if the body could no longer be a good host to the soul, an individual could choose to leave this world. Plotinus' ultimate position on self-homicide is difficult to ascertain, however, because he adamantly opposed falling victim to the passions of grief, disgust and anger. Voluntary death under such circumstances becomes an act based on emotion, not reason. Despite these ambiguities, it seems that Plotinus accepted the Socratic loophole that one could kill oneself after receiving the divine *anangke*.[15]

We cannot know to what degree the various opinions regarding self-homicide in the Greco-Roman world influenced Jesus or his followers. However, it is clear that voluntary death has always been a difficult issue and that there was no clear consensus in the ancient world. Certainly, to conclude that voluntary death was morally ambiguous in the ancient world and that it was turned into a sin by later Christian apologetics would be anachronistic and ahistorical. However, it cannot be stated with surety that voluntary death always was regarded as anathema by the ancients. From time immemorial, people seem always to have disagreed about the manner in which death should be met.

Voluntary death in the Hebrew Bible and the Talmud

My fellow student at Antioch McGregor was certain that explicit prohibitions against voluntary death could be found in the Bible. In fact, there are none in the Tanakh (the Hebrew Bible), the Apocrypha, Rabbinical literature or the Christian New Testament. Perhaps more fascinating is that six cases of voluntary death can be found in the Tanakh: Abimelech (Judges 9:50–57), Saul and his armor bearer (1 Samuel 31), Samson (Judges 16:23–31), Ahithophel (2 Samuel 16:23) and Zimri (1 Kings 16). In none of the accounts is a judgment made upon the individuals because of their manner of death. In fact, the deaths of Saul and his armor bearer related in 1 Sam 31[16] are described as honorable. Saul is given a proper burial in hallowed ground, a right granted only to those deemed worthy (1 Sam 31:13; 2 Sam 21:12–14). Both men take their own lives; had this been deemed anathema, certainly the writer of 1 Samuel would have indicated that such was the case. On the contrary, his burial indicates that his death was honorable.

Exodus 20:13

Exodus 20:13, "You shall not murder," popularly known as the Sixth Commandment, is the most common text cited as a prohibition against suicide. (Christians may be more familiar with the translation "You shall not kill," but the proper rendering of the Hebrew verb is "murder.") This passage must be taken seriously, but it must also be placed within its proper context. While the Ten Commandments (Ex 20:2–17) have been extracted from the Book of Exodus and made to stand on their own, the verses are part of a larger covenant made between the Israelite people and their God. In fact, the Book of Exodus contains a large number of expectations and laws aimed at regulating Israelite society. Ex 21:1–11 concerns the selling of slaves; Ex 22:2 discussed the bloodguilt levied upon a thief.

The laws and regulations found in Exodus were part of an ancient system of laws, many of which are no longer relevant to contemporary society. The Ten Commandments, however, are treated as special, and have been removed from their original context. Most Christians pick and choose what they wish to believe from the Tanakh; this is certainly necessary, given that society and culture have changed greatly, but it is problematic. Emphasizing the Sixth Commandment and condemning those who commit suicide, but ignoring the other prohibitions and rules that regulate trade, marital relationships and filial piety, is special pleading. If it is God's law that one should not kill oneself because of Ex 20:13, why is it not God's law that one should not allow a sorceress to live (Ex 22:18)?

Certainly I am not advocating that contemporary societies begin executions of sorceresses, nor am I saying that the whole of the Bible be rendered irrelevant because every passage cannot be followed literally. The Tanakh is sacred to Jews and Christians, and the writings are a central part of religious observance. The texts must be respected and considered with seriousness. Nevertheless, what I am pointing out is that choices are made; people tend to follow certain rules and regulations and ignore others. It is not appropriate, however, to give undue legitimacy to certain passages over others because of personal preference. If one pericope can be discussed and placed in a new context, other passages must be subject to the same possibilities.

The Book of Joshua and 1 Kings concern the conquest of Canaan, the Promised Land flowing with milk and honey, by the Israelites. But Canaan was not unoccupied. It was home to various groups of people – the Canaanites, Jebusites, Hittites and Amorites – with their own cities, gods, laws and cultures. Under the leadership of Joshua, the Israelite armies marched into various settlements (Jericho, Ai) and slaughtered entire groups of people. Indeed, during the siege of Jericho, God commanded that all the inhabitants be killed, "except Rahab the harlot and all who are with her in her house" (Joshua 6:17; NRSV). This task was carried out, for in Joshua 6:21 it is reported, "Then they [the Israelites] utterly destroyed all in the city, both men and women, young and old, oxen sheep, and asses, with the edge of the sword." What is this, if not murder?

The most common objection to the argument I have presented is that the conquest of Canaan was not murder because it constituted the will of God. It was the divine mandate that the people of Israel be given the Promised Land, and God decreed that the land be conquered through bloodshed. Who are we, the argument goes, to question the will of God. The killings were part of *harem*, the dedication of war spoils to God; the inhabitants and the contents of the city or town were offered as a *holocaust*, or burnt offering, to the Lord. To this I answer: What does such a view say about God? Are some lives more valuable to God than others? Is there justifiable homicide? Or, if one does not consider the deaths of the Canaanites to be homicide, are there certain circumstances in which God believes it is acceptable to kill? If so, why is it not possible that God can lead an individual person to kill him or her self? Why is this outside God's prerogative?

The Sixth Commandment cannot be cited as a proof text for God's abhorrence of voluntary death because it is unclear what constitutes murder. If the wholesale slaughter of entire groups of people is not murder because God commanded it, there must be the possibility that God could command an individual person to end his or her own life. In this case, voluntary death would not be self-murder.

Ultimately, no explicit text condemning voluntary death can be found in all of the Hebrew Bible. The modern term "suicide," with all its pejorative overtones, does not apply to the vast and complicated issue of voluntary death. The Hebrew Bible does not differentiate between the death of Abimelech, who ordered himself killed, or the death of Samson, who killed himself in order to maximize the number of Philistine casualties. In both cases, death was voluntary; the texts do not say that one found favor with God and the other did not. Further-more, arguments that Saul's death was honorable because he died on the battlefield, or that Zimri's voluntary death indicates that God pun-ishes sin by making evil doers kill themselves, are not supported by the texts. No comment upon either death is made by the writers of the texts; we must not put words into their metaphorical mouths.

The Talmud

The Talmud is a collection of Jewish oral law that dates from the second century CE. Technically, the Talmud contains two separate col-lections: *The Babylonian Talmud* and *The Jerusalem Talmud* (also known as *The Palestinian Talmud*). Both were written over the course of many centuries by Jews living in the communities from which the collections derive their names. To become an expert on Talmudic law takes dec-ades – some would even say an entire lifetime – and I certainly am not a Talmud scholar. However, in all my research and discussions with experts on Judaism, I was not able to come across a single passage that prohibits voluntary death.

Although an argument from silence can be presented – the Talmud does not explicitly detail how a person should kill him or her self, therefore one should not – such a position does not hold. The Talmud is an awesome collection of law that regulates the minutiae of life. That voluntary death is wholly absent indicates that there was no universal or established position concerning the issue. It can just as easily be put forth that silence indicates the permissibility of voluntary death; this, of course, is not an acceptable position. We cannot know what the views of second-century Jews were regarding the issue, and therefore, we must pass over it in silence.

Christian persecution of "suicides": an unfortunate irony

An examination of Western civil law, which supposedly finds its basis in the scriptures, reveals that, historically, those who attempt to and/or successfully kill themselves lose their civil rights and human dignity. The definition of voluntary death as a crime comes rather late in the (Catholic) Christian tradition.[17] It was not until the sixth century that voluntary death was decreed illegal, and the only scriptural reference offered to support the ban was an appeal to the Sixth Commandment: "Thou shalt not murder." (See above for discussion.) Christianity spread in the latter half of the first millennium of the Common Era, becoming the foundation upon which much of Western civilization was built. During this time European culture incorporated canon law into civil law.

Consequently, it was illegal to kill oneself in Europe for many centuries. Indeed, a number of people were executed for trying to kill themselves. In nineteenth-century England, a Russian exile, Nicholas Ogarev, witnessed such an execution, and wrote to his mistress to voice his disgust:

> A man was hanged who had cut his throat, but who had been brought back to life. They hanged him for suicide. The doctor had warned them that it was impossible to hang him as the throat would burst open and he would breath through the aperture. They did not listen to his advice and hanged their man. The wound in the neck immediately opened and the man came back to life again although he was hanged. It took time to convoke the aldermen to decide the question of what was to be done. At length the aldermen assembled and bound up the neck below the wound until he died. Oh my Mary, what a crazy society and a stupid civilization.[18]

Today we may be surprised by such behavior, but this anecdote does not describe a unique occurrence. Church and state alike, particularly in Christian Europe, historically have advocated violent punishment of those who try to kill themselves. The purpose, of course, was to act as a public deterrent against suicide. As A. Alvarez remarks in *The Savage God*, "the suicide was as low as the lowest criminal."[19] Ironically, a central element of the Christian story relates a parallel practice that might make Christians uncomfortable with the Church's historical policies toward voluntary death.[20]

Suicide and crucifixion

Many Christians today wear crucifixes around their necks as a sign of their faith; few realize how brutal, humiliating and violent was crucifixion in the ancient world. Jesus of Nazareth was not an anomaly; he was not the only person to ever be crucified. In fact, Josephus informs us that, in 4 CE, 2,000 Jews who participated in a revolt in Syria were crucified by the governor, Varus.[21] Crucifixion originated with the Medes and the Persians; by the time of Alexander the Great during the fourth century BCE, crucifixion was a common Hellenistic practice. It was spread to the Romans during the Punic Wars and was the standard form of execution for slaves, brigands and non-Roman citizens by the time of Jesus. Roman citizens, except on rare occasions, were not crucified; it was reserved for the lowest of the low, the scourge of the occupied societies. There is an abundance of anecdotal evidence from ancient historians and writers such as Cicero, Justinian, Seneca and Josephus that attests to the revulsion and fear people held for crucifixion and for those who were crucified; it was a part of life that, regardless of one's station or social class, could not be ignored.

Fifteen hundred years later, European Christians who wished to send a message that voluntary death was not to be tolerated in their civilized society merely had to imitate the policies of the empire that executed their Messiah. The logic employed by European Christians is startlingly similar: if a failed "suicide" is executed in a manner analogous to the lowest possible criminal, the people will understand that voluntary death is not to be tolerated. In fact, in a chilling parallel to the Jewish practice of "dead crucifixion," the bodies of "suicides" in Elizabethan England were dragged publicly by a horse to a place of "punishment and shame" where the body was hanged and left until the magistrate either took it down or ordered it removed.[22] Like their ancient Palestinian counterparts, European Christians were constantly reminded that crimes against the state, including voluntary death, would be swiftly and publicly punished.

The parallels between those who were crucified during the time of Jesus and the treatment of "suicides" in Europe, from the sixteenth to the nineteenth century, do not end with public desecration of the corpses. Although the evidence is sometimes difficult to interpret, it seems that during the time of Jesus the Roman authorities would have been reluctant to allow one who had been crucified to be given a proper burial. In those cases where it was allowed, a significant bribe usually had to be offered to the right people. Yet even if the crucified person had a relative or friend wealthy enough to retrieve the body from the cross, if the deceased was a Jew, an honorable burial in one's ancestral plot was not possible (1 Kings 13:21–2). However, there is evidence from the Mishnah (a collection of second-century Jewish oral law), that the bones of one interred in a burial ground for the "accursed" could have his bones collected in an ossuary (burial box) and placed into an ancestral burial plot. Whether this privilege was extended to those who were crucified by the Romans is not clear, nor is it clear if this would have been the practice during the time of Jesus.[23]

What is certain is that crucifixion was a barbaric act meant to humiliate the executed and one that resulted, most likely, in the victim being denied a proper burial. Likewise, those who committed self-homicide in Christian-controlled Europe were not allowed to be buried in Church cemeteries, which were understood to be sanctified ground. Oftentimes "suicides" were interred at a crossroads where a stake was driven through the body to prevent the ghost from rising, "as though there were no difference between a suicide and a vampire."[24] This and similar practices continued well into the nineteenth century. Such humiliations and desecrations were made public and condoned by the authorities. Once again, the average person lived by a useful maxim: Message delivered, message received.

Although it can be argued that the Church's prohibition of voluntary death was due to concern for the fate of a "suicide's" soul, the civil government had ulterior motives for advocating a general abhorrence of voluntary death: the estates of those who took their own lives most often reverted to the state or the crown.[25] This may seem like a contradiction, since, logically, in order to maximize its gain, the state would encourage people to kill themselves, but such was not the case. The state had to establish legal precedent for its seizure of land; although democracy had not yet been born in France, nor had the political system of contemporary England been fully adopted, there was still a reverence for due process – the monarch had to act according to law, or face public disfavor.[26] By passing laws that made self-homicide a crime against the state, monarchs gained the power to seize property. This practice, though legal, was not universally favored. The writer Voltaire, bemoaning the state of his contemporary France, notes: "His [the suicide's] goods are given to the King, who almost always grants half of them to the leading lady of the Opera, who prevails upon one of her lovers to ask for it; the other half belongs by law to the Inland Revenue."[27]

One who committed voluntary death, even a member of the aristocracy, faced the posthumous loss of all social status; in England, the family castle was destroyed and the lands seized. Those who were left behind, today called "suicide survivors," would not only have lost their loved one, but would also have been deprived of house and home. One wonders if Shakespeare was aware of this reality when he had Hamlet ask his famous question: "To be, or not to be, that is the question: Whether 'tis nobler in the mind to suffer the slings and arrows of outrageous fortune, or to take arms against a sea of troubles and, by opposing, end them? To die: to sleep."[28] Had Hamlet been English, a voluntary death would have had far-reaching consequences. Even self-homicide for love, as was the case of Shakespeare's young lovers Romeo and Juliet, would have resulted, at the very least, in the brutalization of their corpses. Voluntary death was considered neither romantic nor heroic by those who really mattered, the civil authorities.

When, and why, does voluntary death become anathema? That is the question. In this chapter we have seen, both through personal anec- dotes and historical evidence, that people who kill themselves have frequently been regarded as weak, hell-bound criminals who have no concern for those they leave behind. As such, they deserve to lose their family homes, to be stripped posthumously of any accolades they had garnered in their lifetimes, and to have their corpses publicly brutalized and denied an honorable burial. Undeniably, there is fear and revulsion for those who kill themselves, but where does it come from? Apart from the writings of the Pythagoreans, we cannot find any explicit prohibitions in Greco-Roman society, nor can a prohibition against voluntary death be found anywhere in the Tanakh or the Christian New Testament. It is apparent that Augustine, whose polemic against Judas' voluntary death was quoted in the opening chapter of this book, has no biblical basis and, in fact, he voices an opinion not supported by extant texts. We must ask, was Augustine voicing a minority opinion?

Also in this chapter we have seen a parallel between the ancient method of crucifixion, used to kill the Christian Messiah, Jesus of Nazareth, and later European Christian actions and policies against "suicides." This connection is disturbing because the violent death of Jesus, later qualified by Christian believers as an unequivocal heavenly victory, has lost its potency and has been used by Christians through- out the ages to justify violence against those who sin against God. I argue that Christian abhorrence of suicide is rooted in a hatred of Judas Iscariot; the befouling of suicide corpses by Christians is symbol- ically a desecration of Judas himself: those who kill themselves betray God just as Judas "betrayed" Jesus. As I have already proved, to use the word "betrayal" for what Judas did is mistranslation, reading into the text actions and motives that condemn him. So too I have proved that Christian abhorrence of voluntary death is based on a tradition that comes from outside Scripture, one that caused English aldermen, in the name of Jesus, to hang a man for trying to kill himself.

In the next chapter we examine the Gospel of Matthew, in which Judas Iscariot kills himself. The themes developed in this chapter will come into play when considering how the Matthean community would have understood Judas' death. I have stated that there is no explicit condemnation against voluntary death in the New Testament. To sup- port this thesis, I must prove that the voluntary death of Judas Iscariot in Matthew is not a clear indictment against "suicide."

5   The growth of a myth: Judas in Matthew

Why did our Lord deliberately choose Judas, who, he perfectly knew, was unworthy of the honour, and would be his betrayer? ... How came it that Jesus Christ, knowingly and willingly, preferred Judas to honest and faithful ministers? ... Our Lord expressly intended to prevent future offences, that we may not feel excessive uneasiness, when unprincipled men occupy the situation of teachers in the Church or when professors of the Gospel become apostates. He gave, at the same time, in the person of one man, an instance of fearful defection, that those who occupy a higher rank may not indulge in self-complacency ... Christ did not prefer Judas to devout and holy disciples, but raised him to an eminence from which he was afterwards to fall, and thus intended to make him an example and an instruction to men of every condition and of every age, that no one may abuse the honour which God has conferred upon him, and likewise that, when even the pillars fall, those who appear to be the weakest believers remain steady.

John Calvin[1]

Mark's gospel was written as the specter of war hung over the Roman-occupied territories and blood filled the streets of Jerusalem. The Markan community, wherever it was located, felt the effects of the brutal Roman army which, in the year 70 CE, marched into Jerusalem and put down the Jewish rebellion. When the Temple fell, the Markan community saw the invasion as a sign that the Parousia was imminent: Repent, they said, the end is drawing nigh. There was no need for an established church (*ekklesia*), no sense in appointing leaders; the kingdom of God was at hand and the apocalypse mere moments away. It is safe to say that the Markan community would be surprised that the world is still here and that Jesus has not returned. In a phrase: Mark was wrong.

By 80–85 CE the most likely date of Matthew's authorship, realities had changed. While some Jews wished to rebel against Rome once again – and indeed, in the second century CE, another revolt occurred – the brutal realities of the war years began to give way to an internal Jewish fight over who represented the true Israel. The two most viable options were the Pharisees, who had watched as the priestly caste of the Sadducees were systematically obliterated by the Romans, and the Jesus believers.[2] This explains why, in Matthew's gospel, the chief enemies of Jesus and his followers are the Pharisees; within the milieu in which the Matthean community lived, a contest had arisen about who was the legitimate leader of God's chosen people. It becomes apparent when reading Matthew's gospel that members of the Matthean community had begun to accept that the Parousia, while certainly expected, was not going to come in a matter of days.[3] Therefore, it was necessary to establish order on earth. An organized, legitimate church became a primary objective. When we look at Matthew's gospel, we see a concerted effort to define the nature and function of God's church. Not surprisingly, the authority of the twelve – particularly that of Peter – is highlighted in Matthew; also not surprisingly, Judas Iscariot is painted with a more negative brush, most often to highlight the goodness of Jesus and his eventual vicar.[4]

In this chapter we shall examine the various Matthean pericopes in which Judas appears. Particular attention will be paid to the role of the twelve and to those individuals who emerge as examples of how one is a follower of Jesus. If Judas was chosen by God to be an example to followers of Jesus, as the sixteenth-century reformer John Calvin surmised, does Matthew's gospel support this view? To answer this question, we must examine how the post-Markan evangelist uses and changes the narrative inherited from his or her predecessor.

THE GOSPEL OF MATTHEW

Matthew's gospel opens quite differently from Mark's. When we read Mt 1:1, we are told not that we are going to hear the good news of Jesus the Anointed; rather, we encounter a family tree of this Jesus, whose ancestry harkens back to Abraham and King David. Forty-two generations after Abraham, a certain Joseph, who is a descendant of David, discovers that his betrothed, Mary, is pregnant. To increase the drama, Matthew informs the listener/reader that Mary and Joseph have not consummated their relationship. Joseph is confused as to what to do – for in an honor/shame culture, he cannot be expected to raise another man's child – and he is told by a messenger of the Lord that he should wed Mary. Joseph is informed that Mary has conceived by the holy spirit and remains true. To convince Joseph (and the listener/reader), the messenger in Matthew quotes Isaiah 7:14:

> Behold, a virgin[5] will conceive a child
> and she will give birth to a son,
> and they will name him Emmanuel.

Joseph is convinced and takes Mary as his bride. In Mark, it is possible to see Jesus as illegitimate; in Matthew, he is transformed into a prince, or at least heir to the royal line of King David.

There are two striking features about the birth narrative that relate directly to our topic. First, the Matthean Jesus is understood as a legitimate successor of the Davidic line.[6] This indicates that it is important to the Matthean community that Jesus' authority and rightful place in the traditions of Israel be authentic. Second, Matthew uses an esoteric text as a portent of Jesus' birth. Though Isa 7:14 is now deeply entrenched in the Christian imagination, its historical context is far removed from the one Matthew gives it.[7] It took time for the Matthean birth tradition of Jesus to develop, and more time for an obscure text, Isa 7:14, to be attached to the narrative. This indicates that the Matthean community is Torah-literate and Torah-focused. By establishing a precedent for quoting the Septuagint in order to place Jesus within a purely Jewish context, and by using traditions not found in Mark to depict Jesus in a specific way, Matthew makes it clear that we are not reading about the Markan Jesus. Immediately we must ask: Who is this Matthean Jesus?

Matthew is overwhelmingly concerned with portraying Jesus as the fulfillment of Jewish prophecy. Stephen L. Harris writes:

> More than any other Gospel writer, he presents Jesus' life in the context of the biblical Law and prophecy. Throughout the entire Gospel, Matthew underscores Jesus' fulfillment of ancient prophecies, repeatedly emphasizing the continuity between Jesus and the promises made to Israel, particularly to the royal dynasty of David. To demonstrate that Jesus' entire career, from conception to resurrection, was predicted centuries earlier by biblical writers from Moses to Malachi, Matthew quotes from, paraphrases, or alludes to the Hebrew Scriptures at least 60 times. (Some scholars have detected 140 or more allusions to the Hebrew Scriptures.) Nearly a dozen times, Matthew employs a literary formula that drives home the connection between prophecy and specific events

in Jesus' life: "All this happened in order to fulfill what the Lord declared through the prophet . . .," Matthew writes, then citing a biblical passage to support his contention (1:22–3; 2:15, 23).[8]

The Matthean Jesus, then, is the figure God has been promising throughout the dynamic history of Israel. Jesus is the true Messiah; he is the ultimate authority on the Torah; and he is the supreme authority for the church (*ekklesia*), which must carry on his work until the Parousia. Our task, therefore, is to see how Judas Iscariot fits into this new story.

Jesus and the twelve

In Mark's gospel, narratives involving the twelve are often intercalated with other narratives, usually to make some point about the twelve as a whole or about individual members. Matthew forgoes this pattern; instead, subtle changes are made to the characterization of the twelve, beginning with Mt 4:18–20, the calling of Simon and Andrew:

> (18) As he was walking by the Sea of Galilee, he spotted two brothers, Simon, also known as Peter, and Andrew his brother, throwing their net in the sea, since they were fishermen. (19) And Jesus says to them, "Become my followers and I'll have you fishing for people!" So right then and there they abandoned their nets and followed him.

Matthew immediately identifies Simon as "Peter," whereas Mark does not refer to Peter until 3:16, the commissioning of the twelve. I find this to be significant because, from the outset of Matthew's gospel, Simon is identified as "the rock" even though Jesus has not yet bestowed the nickname upon him.

The role of Andrew is also changed slightly in Mt 4:18, where he is identified as Simon Peter's brother, which Mark's gospel is ambiguous about. This detail may not seem important, but remember that in Mark there is another member of the twelve named Simon: Simon the Zealot.[9] The reader of Mark's gospel cannot be certain that the Simon named in 1:16 is the Peter of 3:16 because Andrew is never named as a brother of "Peter," he is only identified as the brother of "Simon." Matthew clears up this ambiguity, making "Simon Peter" the first disciple/member of the twelve called by Jesus, and declaring that Andrew is his brother. Within the first three chapters of Matthew's gospel, Markan ambiguities regarding the lineage of Jesus and two members of the twelve are clarified.

It is not until Mt 10:1 that the twelve appear as a group and are given authority "to drive out unclean spirits and to heal every disease and every ailment." Once again, Judas Iscariot is named last and described as "the one who, in the end, turned him [Jesus] in" (v.4). This is not a curious element; what is peculiar is that a great deal of material separates the calling of Peter, Andrew, James and John from the commission of the twelve. The listener/reader assumes that the "disciples" who follow Jesus and receive his teachings include the specific individuals named in 4:18–22. In Mark's gospel, the twelve are set aside as a distinct group, which functions in a unique manner, but they are never called the "twelve disciples." In Mt 10:1, however, the twelve are referred to as the "twelve disciples" (*tous dōdēka mathētas*). Thus Matthew has removed the distinction between the disciples and the twelve that existed in Mark's gospel, making the two synonymous. This is a subtle, yet tremendous shift; now the listener/reader, hearing the word "disciples," will think "twelve."

Mt 10 is an important chapter, not only because it utilizes Q passages on how one becomes a follower of Jesus, and places them within the context of the teachings given to the twelve disciples, but also because the specific realities of the Matthean community are apparent. For example, in Mt 10:5–40 (cf. Mk 6:6–13), the twelve are warned about persecution, familial division, and the possible loss of life; however, the hand of the Matthean redactor is strong, particularly in vv.5–6: "Jesus sent out the twelve disciples after he had given them these instructions: 'Don't travel on foreign roads and don't enter Samaritan towns, but go rather to the lost sheep in the house of Israel.'" These verses support the Matthean christology: Jesus has come as a servant of Israel, not of a false-Israel or of non-Torah observant Gentiles. The twelve disciples have been given authority to preach to Israel by the Jewish Messiah. Once again, this is not the Markan Jesus.

Matthew's complete eradication of the distinctions between the twelve and the generic disciples found in Mark's gospel is displayed in Mt 11:1. Jesus finishes instructing the twelve and they go their separate ways. Unlike Mark's gospel, the Matthean twelve do not reconvene (cf. Mk 6:30); rather, they disappear and Jesus is surrounded by "disciples" (*mathētai*) (cf. Mt 12:1–8//Mk 2:23–8; Mt 13:10–17//Mk 4:10–12, etc.). It is difficult for the listener/reader to see "the twelve" as a distinct group, for the defining characteristics found in Mark's gospel have been smoothed over. I think these changes underscore Matthew's desire that the listener/reader see no division between the two. We must ask if this means that the Matthean community accepted the authority of the twelve, and if so, what impact did this have on the community's understanding of how one is a follower of Jesus? I think the answers are to be found by examining two figures: Simon Peter and Judas Iscariot.

The authority of Peter

Matthew highlights the authority of Peter both by subtle changes to Markan material and by the inclusion of special-M traditions. First, let us look at an example of a subtle change to a Markan pericope. In Mk 1:29, Jesus enters the house of Simon and Andrew and heals Simon's mother-in-law. Mt 8:14 tells the same story, but in this account Andrew is removed from the narrative; only Peter and Jesus are present for the healing. Nowhere in Mark's gospel is Peter the only follower of Jesus present when a healing is performed.

Next, let us look at an example of special-M material being inserted into a Markan narrative so as to highlight the authority of Peter. Mt 14:24–33 reads:

> (24) By this time the boat was already some distance from land and was being pounded by waves because the wind was against them. (25) About three o'clock in the morning he came toward them walking on the sea. (26) But when the disciples saw him walking on the sea, they were terrified. "It's a ghost," they said, and cried out in fear. (27) Right away Jesus spoke to them, saying "Take heart, it's me! Don't be afraid." (28) In response Peter said, "Master, if it's really you, order me to come across the water to you." (29) He said, "Come on." And Peter got out of the boat and walked on the water and came toward Jesus. (30) But with the strong wind in his face, he started to panic. And when he began to sink, he cried out, "Master, save me." (31) Right away Jesus extended his hand and took hold of him and says to him, "You don't have enough trust! Why did you hesitate?" (32) And by the time they had climbed into the boat, the wind had died down. (33) Then those in the boat paid homage to him, saying, "You really are God's son."

Matthew retains the narrative framework of Mk 6:24–33 with one major exception: Peter suddenly becomes a central actor. The pericope is curious for at first Peter is able to walk on the water; his faith, it is implied, is strong. However, "with the strong wind in his face" (v.30), Peter sinks into the water and cries out for Jesus to save him. After Jesus pulls him out he says, in v.31, "You don't have enough trust! Why did you hesitate?" Just as in Mark's narrative, members of the twelve lack trust, impairing their ability to perform miracles. Is the listener/ reader meant to identify with Peter? Or with the remaining members of the twelve who rightly identify Jesus? Both? What is Matthew's intent with this passage?

I think that Matthew changes the characterization of Simon Peter for two distinct reasons. First, to establish that there was historically a close relationship between Jesus and Simon Peter, and that Peter is the rightful heir to Jesus' ministry. Second, because Matthew was forced to use Mark's gospel, Matthew must make Simon Peter an example of how one can lose faith yet still be redeemed. This thesis can be proven through an examination of three test cases – pericopes in which Matthew portrays Peter's close relationship with Jesus.

Mt 15:10–18 as a test case: Jesus teaches Peter

The first pericope is Mt 15:10–18, quoted below.

> (10) And he summoned the crowd and said to them, "Listen and try to understand. (11) What goes into your mouth doesn't defile you; what comes out of your mouth does." (12) The disciples came and asked him, "Don't you realize that the Pharisees who heard this remark were offended by it?" (13) He responded: "Every plant which my heavenly Father does not plant will be rooted out. (14) Never mind them. They are blind guides of blind people! If one blind person guides another, both will end up in some ditch." (15) Then Peter replied, "Explain the riddle to us." (16) He said, "Are you still as dim-witted as the rest? (17) Don't you realize that everything that goes into the mouth passes into the stomach and comes out in the outhouse? (18) But the things that come out of the mouth come from the heart, and those things defile a person."

Mt 15:10–18 parallels Mk 7:14–23, but Matthew changes two important details. First, he places the lesson in the context of a conflict with the Pharisees, as is characteristic of this gospel. He says they shall be rooted out, that they are blind guides to blind people, and so on. This detail serves to propel the Matthean agenda that the Jesus believers are the True Israel. Second, Matthew has Peter ask Jesus to explain the riddle (v.15), whereas a generic disciple addresses this question to Jesus in Mark's gospel. Why does Matthew do this? I answer that the purpose is to establish Peter as the one who asks Jesus about teachings. Matthew is forced to use the material available from Mark; in many ways he is constricted, given that so much of the Markan narrative takes a negative stance against the twelve. In Mt 15:10–18, however, Matthew is able to establish a relationship in which Peter directly receives teaching from Jesus. Granted, Peter comes across as dense, yet he also emerges as the one to whom Jesus imparts the secrets of his enigmatic truths.

Mt 16:13–20: Peter is given the keys to the kingdom

The next pericope that involves Peter is Mt 16:13–20 (cf. Mk 8:27–30), in which Jesus asks what people have been saying about him. The Matthean version follows the Markan framework until vv. 17–19, where Jesus says to Peter:

> (17) You are to be congratulated, Simon son of Jonah, because flesh and blood did not reveal this to you but my Father who is in heaven. (18) Let me tell you, you are Peter, "the Rock," and on this very rock I will build my congregation, and the gates of Hades will not be able to overpower it. (19) I shall give you the keys of Heaven's domain, and whatever you bind on earth will be considered bound in heaven, and whatever you release on earth will be considered released in heaven.[10]

Here we find definitive, forensic evidence that the Matthean community accepted the authority of Peter, though not necessarily that of the twelve. Peter is explicitly named as the successor to Jesus, the rightful overseer of the church/congregation (*ekklesia*). He is given power to bind and release things on earth, actions that shall be mirrored in heaven. This passage is special-M material. What this suggests to me is that the Matthean community either had contact with Peter, with one of the twelve who supported the authority of Peter, or with subsequent followers of Peter, perhaps a generation after the death of Jesus. How else does one explain such a radical shift in the characterization of Peter?

Mt 16:21–23: the mutual exorcism is changed

I have argued in Chapter 3 that the most damning evidence against Peter in Mark's gospel comes in Mk 8:31–3, where Peter attempts to exorcize Jesus. Once again, Matthew is forced to use Markan material, and once again, Matthew changes the details to suit the Matthean view of the church (*ekklesia*):

(21) From that time on Jesus started to make it clear to his disciples that he was destined to go to Jerusalem, and suffer a great deal at the hands of the elders and the ranking priests and scholars, and be killed, and on the third day, be raised. (22) And Peter took him aside and began to lecture him, saying, "May God spare you, master; this surely can't happen to you." (23) But he turned and said to Peter, "Get out of my sight, you Satan, you. You are dangerous to me because [*skandalon ei emou*] you are not thinking in God's terms but in human terms."

In Mark's version of this event, no words of Peter are recorded; Peter "rebukes" (*epitiman*) Jesus in an attempt to expel a demon from him. In Matthew, Peter is given words that do not befit an exorcism. Instead, Peter asks that God spare Jesus; there is no longer an exorcism.

In fact, Peter has concern for Jesus, an emotion the Markan Peter lacks completely. Jesus' response to Peter is also significant. Instead of saying, "Get out of my sight, you Satan, you, because you're not thinking in God's terms, but in human terms" (Mk 8:33), the Matthean Jesus says, "Get out of my sight, you Satan you. You are dangerous to me (*skandalon ei emou*) because you are not thinking in God's terms, but in human terms." I think the Matthean wording changes the emphasis of the pericope. Peter is exorcized by Jesus because he, Peter, represents a danger to Jesus because of his compassion, not the fact that he attempted to exorcize Jesus. The listener/reader certainly has sympathy for Peter, who wants only to protect his Messiah.

Mt 26:40–41: a rock until the end

In Mt 26:40–41, Peter's authority is subtly, but undeniably, left intact, thereby changing an important detail of Mark's gospel.

(40) And he returns to the disciples and finds them sleeping, and says to Peter, "Couldn't you stay awake with me for one hour? (41) Be alert, and pray that you won't be put to the test! Though the spirit is willing, the flesh is weak."

Matthew retains the Markan framework for the narrative; in v.35 "all of them" take the oath of fealty (once again, we must presume that Judas is present). Matthew also retains Mark's wording for Jesus' agony in Gethsemane. There is, however, an important redactional change in v.40: Jesus does not address Simon Peter as "Simon," as he does in Mark's narrative. I have argued that this detail represents the Markan community's rejection of Peter's authority. Conversely, Matthew's removal of this detail is meant to indicate that Jesus, knowing Peter will deny him, still affirms Peter's authority as the "rock" upon which the church will be built. Jesus must affirm this because the Matthean community affirms it. Suddenly, Peter has become the archetype of one who loses faith but is able to regain it.

There is no doubt in my mind that the Matthean community accepted the authority of the twelve. It is also clear to me that Peter as an arche-type for faith begins with Matthew's subtle changes to Mark's narrative. Our task, though, is not to examine Peter, but Judas Iscariot. Therefore, we must see how Judas functions in Matthew's gospel and how he functions as a disciple.

JUDAS: "WHAT ARE YOU WILLING TO PAY ME IF I TURN HIM OVER TO YOU?"

In Mt 26:3–5, the conspiracy against Jesus is finally unleashed.

> (3) Then the ranking priests and the elders of the people gathered in the courtyard of the high priest, whose name was Caiaphas, (4) and they conspired to seize Jesus by trickery and kill him. (5) Their slogan was: "Not during the festival, so there won't be a riot among the people."

The fate that Jesus has been promising is about to unfold. "How will it happen?" the listener/reader wonders, all the while knowing that Judas Iscariot has to play some role, given his introduction in Mt 10. Sure enough, in 26:14, Judas appears. However, this seems a much different Judas to the one we encountered in Mark.

> (14) Then one of the twelve, Judas Iscariot by name, went to the ranking priests (15) and said, "What are you willing to pay me if I turn him over to you?" They agreed on thirty silver coins. (16) And from that moment he started looking for the right occasion to turn him in.

Matthew retains the basic Markan language of introduction, but it is Judas who suggests that money change hands. A motive is finally provided to Judas: greed. Such is the characteristic that Christians his-torically have attached to Judas Iscariot. But is this what Matthew intended to convey?

The specific amount of thirty silver coins is interesting. Ex 21:32 states that thirty *shekelim* is the going rate for a slave gorged by a bull; similarly, during the time of Jesus, thirty silver pieces (whether *shekelim* or *drachmae*) was the average price for a slave or lower-class person.[11] By no means would this amount have made Judas wealthy. Is the point, then, that Judas was so consumed with avarice that he sold Jesus for a paltry amount? Or is the reader/listener supposed to react to Jesus' being sold for the price of a slave? In other words: is Matthew making a christological statement? Is Jesus' fulfillment of Scripture understood as freeing us from slavery?[12] That Matthew, and only Matthew, mentions the specific amount of thirty silver pieces is significant (as we shall see in Mt 27:3), but given the evidence available to us, the significance is not yet discernible. What is interesting, though, is that the Matthean Judas is already a more developed character than his Markan counterpart. According to Matthew, Judas seeks payment for a specific service. We must ask: would a Jewish man acting as an informer for Temple officials have been abnormal in the ancient world?

The informer

Long before the play *The Informer* by Bertolt Brecht or the song of the same name by the rapper Snow, the informer was considered a regular and necessary part of ancient government. During the time of Jesus, Roman politics provided a chilling foreshadowing of McCarthyism in twentieth-century United States: any comment or perceived slight to the status quo could open one to prosecution.[13] Friends turned upon friends, family members upon family members. While the central political intrigues of Rome were carried out far from the occupied Jewish homeland, the role of the informer was not absent from the Jewish milieu. In Hebrew, the word *masor* or *maser*, used to describe one who informs, appears infrequently in the Hebrew Bible,[14] but is more common in later Hebrew writings.

Interestingly enough, the term is closely related to the Greek *paradidōmi*, and properly means one who "hands over" or "delivers" property, people or information. William Klassen writes:

> The masor or maser hands over a person or property from the inside to the outside, or from the inner circle to the outer. An act such as this may be accompanied by betrayal or treachery, but neither is implied in the word. The best English translation of this word may well be placed on a continuum from delator or denouncer to informer. An informer need not, however, have

anything to do with betrayal and may, in fact, render an essential service. Police officers, a relatively new invention of civilization, are paid informers in that it is their duty to report infractions of the law or anything that threatens society to those who can do something about it. Accordingly, from ancient times, they have been called "peace officers."[15]

There has been much imaginative speculation regarding the motives of Judas in "handing over" Jesus to the authorities. While some explanations might be intriguing, to be sound they must be rooted in the information afforded the listener/reader. One theory in particular warrants our attention. The biblical scholar Frank Morrison argues that Judas was authorized by Jesus to inform the authorities that he, Jesus, was ready to be arrested. Morrison writes: "Jesus was a master of psychology, and His irrevocable determination to deliver Himself to His accusers that night was accomplished by infinitely subtler means."[16] That Jesus explicitly told Judas to hand him over is mere conjecture; I also reject the anachronistic language of "psychology." However, Morrison may point us toward the Matthean community's understanding of Jesus' arrest. If the Jesus event is to be placed primarily within the context of Scripture fulfillment, is Judas' role not one of necessity? Once again, Matthew is forced to use the Markan account of Judas' role in the arrest. However, Matthew attaches new details: Judas seeks out the Temple priests and promises to hand Jesus over for the price of a slave. Given the necessity of Jesus' arrest for his expiative death, would the Matthean community have seen Judas' act as perfidious?

I do not think there is a definitive answer. From what we are told, Judas' motivation is money, yet the amount is not large, thus causing the listener/reader to pay particular attention to it. What Judas does – the act of informing on Jesus and also being the agent who hands him over – was a constituent part of both Roman and Jewish cultures, one that did not entail betrayal or treachery. From the information we have, it cannot be assumed that there is malice in the Matthean Judas' actions, nor can it be assumed that there is benevolence; we simply do not know why Judas does what he does. Consequently, if Judas is being presented as an archetype or example of discipleship, it seems unclear how the listener/reader is expected to regard him.

The Passover meal

Mt 26:17–25, the Passover meal, is an important text concerning Judas and his relationship to Jesus:

(17) On the first [day] of Unleavened Bread the disciples came to Jesus and said, "Where do you want us to get things ready for you to celebrate Passover?" (18) He said, "Go into the city to so-and-so and say to him, 'The teacher says, "My time is near, I will observe Passover at your place with my disciples" '." (19) And the disciples did as Jesus instructed them and they got things ready for Passover. (20) When it was evening, he was reclining [at the table] with his twelve followers. (21) As they were eating, he said, "So help me, one of you is going to turn me in." (22) And they were very upset and each one said to him in turn, "I'm not the one, am I, Master?" (23) In response he said, "The one who dips his hand in the bowl with me—that's who's going to turn me in! (24) The son of Adam departs just as the scriptures predict, but damn the one responsible for turning the son of Adam in. It would be better for that man had he never been born!" (25) Judas, who was to turn him in, responded, "You can't mean me, can you rabbi? (*Mēti egō eimi, Rabbi*) [literally, "Not I am, Rabbi]" He says to him, "You said it."

In Mt 26:17–25, Judas' conference with the priests is followed by the preparation for the Passover Supper, retaining the framework of Mk 14:12. There is a subtle difference, however: in Mark 14:13, two of Jesus' disciples (*duō tōn mathētōn autou*) are sent to make the preparations; in the parallel Matthean passage (26:19), the disciples (*mathētai*) as a group make the preparations. As I noted above, Matthew has constructed the gospel so that the listener/reader understands the "twelve" and the "disciples" to be synonymous. Indeed, in Matthew the twelve disciples are the only ones present at the Passover meal, a detail that is ambiguous in Mark's narrative. In Matthew, Jesus and the twelve disciples are the principal actors, providing more evidence that the Matthean community supported an organized, hierarchical church structure.

As in Mark, the Matthean Jesus informs his disciples that one from their number will hand him in (v.21). Once again, they are upset and individuals enquire whether they might be the ones who will perform this act. Verse 23 retains Mark's detail that the dipping[17] action demarcates the one who will turn Jesus in. Instead of describing this action, Matthew inserts v.25, in which Judas implicates himself. This has a powerful effect. Unlike Mark's gospel, which suggests that any of the twelve are capable of turning Jesus is, Matthew highlights the fact that Judas is the one; the deficient nature of the other eleven is not highlighted.

The Matthean Passover meal in vv.27–30 continues much like the Markan meal, with one essential difference. In v.28, Jesus says, in reference to the wine as his blood, "this is the blood of the covenant, which has been poured out for many for the *forgiveness of sins*" (my italics). Since Mark lacks this christological element, the addition is immensely important. The Matthean community understood Jesus' death to be expiative and one that results in the forgiveness of sins. Judas partook of the wine. Does this detail imply that Judas is forgiven?

We must be careful not to read too much into Judas' participation in the Eucharist. From what we have discovered, there is no evidence to show that Judas' action of handing over Jesus to the authorities was originally understood as a sin. The act has been made into a sin by later Christian communities. Nevertheless, we must allow the detail to stand on its own. That Jesus does not prevent Judas from participating produces important theological and soteriological ramifications.

The kiss of peace

Unfortunately, Mt 26:49–50 is a pericope that has received an undue amount of attention.

> (49) And he came right up to Jesus, and said, "Hello, Rabbi," and kissed him. (50) But Jesus said to him, "Look friend, what are you doing here?"

Some exegetes have been uncomfortable with the potentially homosexual nature of the kiss between Judas and Jesus, arguing that it certainly was not a kiss on the lips, and was possibly a kiss on the hand. Such conjecture is both silly and unnecessary: one need only look at Middle Eastern cultures today, in which men readily kiss one another upon the lips, not in an act of sexuality but of friendship. (It is sometimes referred to as the kiss of peace.) One should not focus on such an insignificant detail, but on the nature of the conversation Matthew reports occurring between Judas and Jesus in v.50.

There are details concerning the text that should be examined, but Jesus' response to Judas in v.50 is problematic. The Greek reads: *etaire, eph' (h)o parei.* This is a difficult line to translate. It can be rendered as some form of a question, as it is above; as an exclamation, given that the vocative and accusative cases have the same endings; or as a statement. Each translation provides a different nuance. Compare: "Friend, for this then you have come!" and "Friend, is this what you come for?" As biblical Greek has no punctuation marks, it is difficult to determine how Matthew intended the passage to be read. Knowing this might be able to provide insight into the Matthean Judas.

I think the importance of the arrest and its lesson to the Matthean community is revealed in v.52. Verses 50b–51 parallel Mark: as the authorities arrest Jesus, an unidentified companion of Jesus draws his sword and cuts off the ear of the high priest's slave. However, v.52 is special-M material: Jesus stops the action, saying "Put your sword back where it belongs. For everyone who takes up the sword will be done in by the sword." The Markan language is once again resumed in v.53, but the shift is significant, however. I argue that v.52 reflects how the Matthean community expected its adherents to behave when arrested: do not rely upon violence, for those who do will fall victim to it; instead, trust that vindication will come. Judas' act is not a central focus of the Matthean arrest account.

Summary

In the Gospel of Matthew Judas evolves as a character. Though still named last in the list of the twelve, the Matthean Judas is less of a one-dimensional character: he is provided with a possible motive (receiving thirty silver coins) for his actions. Understanding the significance of his motives is difficult; however, the amount was roughly equivalent to the purchase price of a slave. If Judas was motivated by greed, Matthew has portrayed him as especially perfidious. If, on the other hand, the significance is christological, we must ask if Judas' role holds any particular importance.

It seems clear to me that Matthew's community was led by an hierarchical, organized group that in some way received its authority from Peter. How else do we explain the bestowal of the keys to the kingdom to Peter, if not as an explicit support of his authority? Through the reordering of Markan material and the incorporation of special-M traditions, Matthew's gospel softens the condemnation of the "twelve." Anonymous disciples disappear in Matthew's gospel in favor of an overwhelming emphasis upon the "twelve," who are understood as synonymous with "disciples." We should not underestimate the importance of this detail. Proper discipleship was understood as staying true to the words of Jesus, favoring non-violence, participating in the community and following hierarchical leadership. According to the Matthean community, Jesus fulfilled the relevant Hebrew scriptures that pertained to the Messiah; in their stead Jesus left his own commandments, a central one being the importance and leadership of Peter. Any controversy over Jesus' paternity is removed in Matthew's gospel, and Simon Peter's relationship with Andrew is made clear.

Matthew was forced to use the Judas tradition; its prevalence was far too great to ignore. Yet Matthew underplays the wholesale condemnation of the twelve and instead focuses the attention upon Peter and Judas. Peter is the premier disciple who, although fallible, has the authority of Jesus. The role of Judas is not so clear; conclusions as to how the Matthean community regarded him are difficult to draw. Even if we accept that the community believed Judas' motive to be greed, the community's soteriology clearly holds that the drinking of the Eucharist wine results in the forgiveness of sins. Judas' actions cannot properly be understood as sinful; but, even if they are, is it not implied that Judas was forgiven when Jesus allowed him to participate in the Eucharist?

As I mentioned in Chapter 3, I hold that Judas Iscariot is a mythological creation of the Markan community. It is clear to me how Judas is meant to function within Mark's narrative. Less apparent, however, is how Judas fits into Matthew's gospel. As I will argue below, I think the significance of Judas is to be found in his death.

The death of Judas Iscariot in Matthew

Judas disappears from Mark's gospel after turning Jesus in. In Mt 27:3–5, however, the reader learns the fate of Judas. In many ways, Christianity has never been the same since.

> (3) Then Judas, who had turned him in,[18] realizing that he had been condemned, was overcome with remorse (*metameletheis*) and returned the thirty silver coins to the ranking priests and elders (4) with this remark, "I have made the grave mistake of turning in this blameless man" But they said, "What's this to us? That's your problem!" (5) And hurling the silver into the temple he slunk off, and went out and hanged himself.

For centuries, Christians have been fascinated by the death of Judas Iscariot. A common consensus is that Judas received his just deserts; his shameful death was befitting of his shameful life. As we have discovered, however, it is unclear that Judas, even if he was an historical figure, lived a shameful life; his handing over of Jesus was not a betrayal, and his being an informer (*masor*) was a constituent part of Jewish and Roman life. Furthermore, as we discussed in the previous chapter, holding that voluntary death is always shameful is not a tenable position. We must ask if Judas' hanging himself would have been considered an honorable death, given Mt 27:3–5.

When objections to Judas' characterization are raised (such as those made in the above paragraph), those who are intent on vilifying Judas fall back on the position that Judas is damned because he does not repent. Karl Barth writes, "According to the NT view, no promise of grace could be held out for Judas, and no genuine penitence was possible."[19] This view is nuanced and is based largely on semantics; as such, I think it is ultimately incorrect. Judas performs three deeds that can be understood as acts of contrition. One, he recognizes he has acted incorrectly; in essence, he changes his mind. The Greek verb *metamelētheis* is used to describe Judas' change of heart; the word refers to a conscious decision, one made over time. It must be noted that *metamelētheis* does not mean "repent." Had Matthew wanted to suggest that Judas repented, the verb *metanoeō* would have been used. It has been argued that the lack of *metanoeō* is evidence that Judas' soul was not saved. This statement, however, cannot with justice be given credence. It presupposes a system of (Christian) penitence that was not in place in the time of Judas; furthermore, if it is true that those who directly sinned against Jesus were required to "repent," Peter would also be condemned, for he does not "repent" after denying Jesus three times. In fact, the only thing Peter does is break down and weep (*epibalōn eklaien*).

The key to understanding Judas' change of heart is identifying his sin: handing over a blameless man to an unjust death. The act of handing Jesus over (*paradidōmi*) is in itself not a sin ((*h*)*amartia*); rather, the sin is that the action results in the shedding of innocent blood. In v.4, Judas declares Jesus to be blameless, further developing the Tale of the Innocent Sufferer; Jesus is so pure that even the person indirectly responsible for the unjust death recognizes Jesus' innocence. It is also significant that the phrase "innocent blood" (*aima athoon*) is not found much in ancient writings; in Hebrew law, the one responsible for handing over or the shedding of innocent blood has committed a serious transgression.[20] Klassen writes, "The only possible atonement under Jewish law when innocent blood is shed or handed over is for someone to die."[21]

Judas performs a second act that indicates contrition in v.5, where he returns the money to the temple. By disassociating himself from the money used to purchase innocent blood, Judas symbolically rejects his role in the event. Evidence from the Mishnah suggests that deals were often invalidated when one party returned money to the Temple. The other party, upon learning that the deal had been nullified, would be required to return the purchased property.[22] By returning the money, Judas signifies that he recognizes his guilt, and repudiates anything connected with the unjust death of Jesus. Many reject this reading, suggesting that Judas' action is not one of contrition, but of misplaced expectations. Brown writes,

> Besides this awe of blood that would have been very convincing to those who share Matt's theology, one can mention a point that may be more convincing to modern readers, namely, that Judas has come to the chief priests, Jesus' enemies, seeking a form of absolution from his sin. He has not sought out Jesus, who had forgiven many sinners; and thus one may well suspect that in the psychology of the Matthean story his remorse has not really meant belief.[23]

Such a reading is difficult to substantiate. We must ask what Brown means by "belief"? Belief in Jesus as the Messiah? This is not the issue at hand; rather, it is whether Jesus is "innocent blood." What would compel Judas to go to such extremes if not a belief that Jesus is truly "innocent blood"? What would drive Judas to end his own life if not a deeply held conviction that he had played a role in an unjust act? I find Brown's objection weak and unsustainable.

Another problem arises when examining v.5. As it is translated above, Judas hurls the money into the Temple; however, Matthew uses *naos*, the word for "the sanctuary," which, historically, was an area within the Temple accessible only to priests. How would Judas have gained access to this area? One can argue that Matthew did not know Temple customs, but given the knowledge of Torah and Jewish customs found in Matthew's gospel, a cognitive dissonance arises when one objects to an ignorance of Temple practices. I think v.5 is evidence that the entire passage is the result of a deliberate attempt to "fulfill" Hebrew prophecy.[24]

Mt 27:9 states that Judas' act fulfills a prophecy found in Jeremiah; this is incorrect. The passage cited by Matthew is found in Zechariah 11:12–13, quoted below (my italics).

> (12) I then said to them, "If it seems right to you, give me my wages; but if not, keep them." So they weighed out as my wages *thirty shekels of silver*. (13) Then the Lord said to me, *"Throw it into the treasury"*—this lordly price *at which I was valued by them. So I took thirty shekels of silver and threw them into the treasury in the house of the Lord.*[25]

The connection to the Potter's Field (v.7) and the Bloody Field (v.8) are discussed below. For the present it will suffice to point out that the whole of Mt 27:5, 9–10 directly parallels Zec 11:12–13. Suddenly, the price of thirty silver coins, the priests offering that price, and the casting of the money into the treasury – all special-M details – make sense. It seems obvious that the author of Matthew, recalling the Zechariah passage from memory, constructed the Judas tale and erroneously attributed the prophecy to Jeremiah.

Judas' third act of contrition is his voluntary death. Recognizing that he has played a role in the spilling of innocent blood, Judas kills himself out of remorse. As I noted above, this was the expected result of such an action. But Judas' voluntary death also further develops the Tale of the Innocent Sufferer: even the one indirectly responsible for the Innocent's death recognizes the truth and cannot bear to have been a part of the unjust death. By the standards of Greco-Roman philosophy, it can be argued that Judas saw his shame as the divine *anangke*. Precedent for such a death can also be found in the Hebrew scriptures. Ahithophel, a general for David who had defected to the side of Absalom, hangs himself out of shame after learning that his advice will not be taken (2 Sam 17:23); unable to face a life in which his opinion is not heeded, he takes his own life.[26] That both Ahithophel and Judas Iscariot hang themselves out of shame is significant; however, there is only a tenuous connection between the two narratives. The two types of shame are different: Ahithophel feels his honor has been so sullied that he cannot continue to live, while Judas takes his life because his actions have resulted in a dishonorable death for Jesus. In comparing the two, all that can be surmised is that, between the years c. 300 BCE and c. 33 CE voluntary death as a way of avoiding shame was acceptable. The authors of neither 2 Sam nor Matthew make any negative comment about the voluntary deaths; there is no evidence that the actions were considered sinful in any way. In fact, it seems that Judas' voluntary death is the only logical and meaningful conclusion.

It is also significant that Judas' change of heart is contrasted with the Temple officials' continued hatred of Jesus. In v.4a Judas makes the strong statement that Jesus is a blameless man. The ranking priests and elders answer Judas by telling him that they are unconcerned; in crude terms, they say "that sounds like a personal problem." Judas attempts to rectify the situation by killing himself; the priests, on the other hand, show no remorse:

(6) The ranking priests took the silver and said, "It wouldn't be right to put this into the temple treasury, since it's blood money." (7) So they devised a plan and bought the Potter's Field as a burial ground for foreigners. (8) As a result, that field has been known as

the Bloody Field even to this day. (9) So the prediction Jeremiah the prophet made came true: "And they took the thirty silver coins, the price put on a man's head (this is the price they put on him among the Israelites), (10) and they donated it for the Potter's Field, as my Lord commanded me."

The priests display no concern for the death of Jesus, nor do they have any sympathy for Judas; their primary objective is to ensure that money used to purchase a death does not infect the Temple (cf. Deut 19:18; 23:19). The contrast between Judas and the priests is undeniable; Judas acts out of remorse, the priests out of concern for Jewish law. The real villains of the narrative never display any emotion that can be construed as positive. How Judas emerged as the guilty one is baffling.

The connection between the Potter's Field (v.7), the Bloody Field (v.8) and the "Jeremiah" prophecy (vv.9–10) is difficult to understand. Scholars have argued that the Potter's Field is rooted in Jer 19:1–13, where the prophet Jeremiah brings the people toward the Valley of Hinnom through the Potsherd Gate (which leads out of the Potters' Quarter) and curses them for having worshiped the pagan Baal. A potter's jug is broken as a symbol of God casting judgment upon the people: they are cast out of Israel and condemned to the Valley of Slaughter, where they die, alienated from their land and their God. However, establishing direct connections between Jer 19:1–13 and Mt 27:7–10 is difficult. Possibly the severed relationship found in Mt 27:7–10 would be that of God and Judas, but if such is the case, why does Jesus refer to Judas as "friend" in Mt 26:50 and why is Judas described as having contrition in Mt 27:3–5? A more distinct possibility is that the severed relationship is between God and the ranking priests, who offered Judas the blood money and use it to purchase a field that calls up images of Jer 19:1–13. Such an interpretation is more in line with the characterization of the ranking priests and the Pharisees in Matthew's gospel.

Other problems arise when attempting to unpack the tenuous connections between Mt 27:7–10 and Jer 19:1–13. In the latter, it is clear that the place is an area of the Kidron valley that was the site of "the burial ground of the common people" (2 Kings 23:6).[27] Those people rejected by the monarch would be buried in this area. In Matthew's gospel, however, it is unclear who the "foreigners" (v.7) buried in the Bloody Field would have been, given that burial of Gentiles would have been a Roman concern, not a Jewish one.[28] The suggestion that Judas himself became a foreigner after his death and was buried in the field is also impossible to substantiate; Matthew does not say that Judas was buried in the Potter's Field, just that it was purchased and then became known as "Bloody Field." No blood is spilled in a hanging; most likely the reference is to "blood money." From Matthew's account, the field is a contemporary (first-century) reality (v.8). Brown writes that "Matt records that the field has been called 'Field of Blood' to this day and so indicates an early origin for the story."[29] This is special pleading: all that can be established is that the field's name had been known for a while, not that the Judas story itself had an early origin. One need only go to any small town and ask for the local folklore concerning a specific site; invariably, several different versions will be given. While the name is known, the origins are not so easy to identify.

CONCLUSIONS

As we shall see in the next chapter, Luke–Acts gives an entirely different account of Judas' death (and, indeed, a wholly different characterization of Judas as a person). Matthew's account, with its muddled references to Jeremiah and Zechariah, seems a deliberate construction. Matthew's propensity to connect events surrounding the Jesus event with the fulfillment of Scripture, particularly in reference to Jeremiah, whom he names specifically three times (something done by no other gospel writer), leads me to believe that there are no historical elements in the death account of Judas. The Bloody Field (called the "Acre of Blood" in Luke–Acts) is a matter of folklore, not history.

Even if one rejects my theory that Judas Iscariot is not an historical figure, let us look at what we know about his depiction in Matthew. Judas is a member of Jesus' chosen twelve; it is never reported that he performed any better or any worse than the other disciples. Consequently, their successes are Judas' successes; their failures are his failures. Unlike the Markan Judas, the Judas in Matthew approaches the ranking priests and asks them for thirty silver pieces. If this is historical, Judas' motive can hardly be described as greed: Jesus is purchased for the price of a slave. More likely, the specific amount of thirty silver pieces comes from Zec 11:12–13. Even if it does not, Judas returns the money as an act of contrition. He also expresses his wrongdoing, declares Jesus to be wholly innocent, and hangs himself in an act of atonement. There is no evidence in either the Hebrew scriptures or the New Testament to suggest that Judas' voluntary death would have been an intrinsically reviled act. On the contrary, more evidence from Hebrew scriptures and relevant Greco-Roman documents shows that, under the circumstances, Judas' voluntary death would have been both expected and regarded as the logical consequence.

One cannot remove Simon Peter from an analysis of Judas Iscariot; both figures change dramatically in Matthew's gospel. Simon Peter is described as having a close relationship with Jesus, is declared the legitimate earthly authority in Mt 16:17–19, and remains "rock" until the end, even though he denies Jesus and is called an oppressor (Satan). Peter emerges as the unchallenged leader of the twelve in Matthew's gospel, and through subtle redaction, Judas, in his final act, is no longer a member of the twelve. I find that there is overwhelming evidence that the Matthean community supported the authority of Peter and his retinue.

Finally, it seems clear to me that the ones who remain guilty until the end in Matthew's gospel are the ranking priests with whom Jesus interacts. They display no remorse for their deeds, and are assiduous in their efforts to rid themselves of the supreme nuisance, Jesus. I certainly am not advocating an anti-Semitic reading of Matthew's gospel; on the contrary, the ranking priests do not represent the Jews as a whole, nor does the rabble who call upon them the "Blood Curse" in Mt 27:25.[30] Matthew does not reject "Jews," but rather rejects any way of being Jewish that does not recognize Jesus of Nazareth's fulfillment of Jewish prophecy and Scripture. Matthew saw Jesus as the fulfillment of God's divine plan. Unfortunately, Matthew's gospel has been misread for centuries, both in terms of the Jews and Judas Iscariot himself.

6 Luke–Acts: Judas as Satan

> The universe is deathless,
> Is deathless because, having no finite self,
> It stays infinite.
> A sound man by not advancing himself
> Stays the further ahead of himself,
> By not confining himself to himself
> Sustains himself outside himself:
> By never being an end in himself
> He endlessly becomes himself.
>
> Lao Tzu[1]

The New Testament writings provide us with various views of Jesus. From the epistles of Paul to Revelation, we encounter many different interpretations of Jesus and his life. Unfortunately, as the centuries of institutionalized Christian hegemony indelibly affected both the social and religious sensibilities of the West, a proper understanding of the Bible became increasingly more difficult. Church councils and Imperial Diets dictated the official view of Jesus, while the scriptures themselves were clouded in a veil of secrecy.

Perhaps no writing in the whole of the Christian canon fell victim to this process more than Luke–Acts, a two-part story separated in the canon by the Gospel of John. The first part, properly called a gospel, traces the life of Jesus, not from a humble beginning in a shack, but as the essential element in the historical drama of Israel that began with the creation of Adam and, as told in the second half of the story, the book of Acts, continues into the life of the church. The writer of Luke informs the reader from the outset that the intention of the two-part story is to write an orderly account (*katēchēthēs logōn*) for a certain Theophilus. This implies not just getting the order of Jesus' life correct, but the proper ordering of history as well. God has a plan, Luke–Acts assures us, and we can see it unfold.

The last of the Synoptic gospels to be written, Luke contains the most polished Greek prose. The account is also the most ambitious of the three, given that it recasts the history of Israel in terms of the Jesus event and emphasizes, in Acts, the shift of religious significance away from Jerusalem and toward Rome. In all likelihood, the Lukan community was less Jewish and more Hellenized than their Matthean counterparts.[2] Characteristic of Luke's gospel is a cosmic battle between good and evil; Satan is a primary figure in the narrative.

In this chapter we shall look at Judas in the Gospel of Luke, focusing primarily upon how the True Israel is defined by the Lukan community and upon the role that Satan plays within the community. The Judas who emerges in this narrative is fundamentally different from his Markan and Matthean counterparts, raising important questions. The most profound difference, however, is in Judas' death, related in the first chapter of Acts.

LUKE–ACTS: RECASTING THE HISTORY OF ISRAEL

The whole of Luke's gospel rotates on a dual axis: recasting the history of Israel to define Gentile Jesus-believers as part of God's chosen people, and imparting to the listener/reader the significant stakes being fought for in the cosmic battle between God and Satan. These two themes can be detected immediately in the opening of Luke's gospel. In 1:11–20 God's angel Gabriel visits Zecheriah, the father of John the Baptizer; in vv.30–38, Gabriel visits the Virgin Mary; and in 2:8–14, an unnamed heavenly messenger, accompanied by a "whole troop of the heavenly army," visits three shepherds and tells them to go visit the newly born Savior. The presence of heavenly beings establishes for the listener/reader that the forces of God are present and active in the Jesus event. The angels are also used to redefine the history of Israel: tales central to the Hebrew Bible are reinterpreted and recast in light of Jesus and those who surround him.

Take, for example, the significant parallels between the births of John the Baptizer and Jesus, and those of Isaac, son of the patriarch Abraham and the matriarch Sarah (Gen 21:1), and Samuel, son of Elkanah and Hannah (1 Sam 1–2). First, the similarities between Isaac and John. According to Genesis, Sarah had "stopped having the periods of women" (18:11b) and was childless until God intervened on her behalf. When Sarah was told that she would become pregnant she did not believe, to which God responded, "Is anything too wondrous for the Lord?" (18:14a). Of course, she was made pregnant and gave birth to Isaac, a central figure in Israel's history and one with whom God promised to make an everlasting covenant (Gen 18:21).

The story of Elizabeth, John the Baptizer's mother, is related in similar terms. Prior to John's birth, Elizabeth was childless, "infertile . . . [and] well along in years" (Lk 1:7), only to be made pregnant with a child central to Israel: "And he will cause many of the children of Israel to turn to the Lord their God" (Lk 1:16). The connection is easily made by the listener/reader: just as God intervened to bring Isaac to ancient Israel, once again God is intervening to bring John the Baptizer to the New Israel, the largely Gentile community of Luke. This is made explicit when the heavenly messenger visits the Virgin Mary and informs her that Elizabeth is pregnant, saying: " 'She who was said to be infertile is already six months along, *since nothing is impossible with God*'" (1:36b–37; my italics). There is a nearly verbatim use of Sarah's language from Genesis: once again, God is active and makes the impossible possible. The Lukan community would have been familiar with the story of Sarah's pregnancy and the importance of Isaac; the similarities would not have been lost upon them.

Second, the parallels between the birth of Samuel and Jesus. Although Hannah and the Virgin Mary became pregnant in different ways, there is a direct parallel. Upon hearing that she is pregnant, Mary recites what is known as the Magnificat (1:46–55), a song of exultation offered to the Lord. This passage is so closely related to the Song of Hannah, found in 1 Sam 2, that there is no doubt that the parallels were intentional. The message is clear: the whole of Israel's history is being repeated in the Jesus event, shifting the emphasis of God's salvific action from the ancient to the new. This is made even more apparent in 3:23–38, where Luke reports that Jesus' lineage can be traced back to Adam.

When we discuss the significance of the Gospel of Luke, it is important to keep in mind the above-mentioned details. As we shall see, although Luke used a great deal of the available Q and Markan material, the gospel dramatically reinterprets the Jesus story to emerge with a Jesus and an understanding of community not found in Q, Mark or Matthew. In my opinion, the Lukan community came under heavy persecution, particularly in the second century, when Acts was written, causing the standards of discipleship to change once again. While the role of Judas in Matthew is ambiguous, I argue that the Lukan Judas clearly serves as the prototype for improper discipleship, since he chooses Satan over Jesus and is struck down by God as a punishment.

The Lukan twelve: discipleship within a gentile Israel

The role of the twelve in Luke's gospel is difficult to evaluate because many subtle changes in the narrative directly contradict my earlier theories regarding the twelve in Mark and Matthew. It is my task to address these issues and attempt to provide satisfactory answers.

In 5:4–8, the calling of Simon Peter incorporates special L material, changing the tone and significance of the call. Simon is not called by word, but by action; Jesus performs a miracle in vv.5–7, causing an abundance of fishes to appear in an empty net. Verse 8 follows: "At the sight of this, Simon Peter[3] fell to his knees in front of Jesus and said, 'Have nothing to do with me Master, heathen that I am'." In the first interchange with Jesus, Simon declares himself unfit to follow Jesus, a detail not found in either Mark or Matthew. Not only is the history of Israel and the nature of Jesus' ministry different in Luke, so too is Peter; he is humble, admitting his own sin and unworthiness.

> (13) The next day, he called his disciples [*mathētas*] and selected twelve [*dōdeka*] of them, whom he named apostles [*apostolous*]: (14) Simon, whom he nicknamed Rock, and Andrew his brother, and James and John, and Philip and Bartholomew, (15) and Matthew, and Thomas, and James the son of Alphaeus, and Simon who was called the Zealot (16) and Judas the son of James,[4] and Judas Iscariot, who turned traitor.

The calling of the twelve (6:13–16) is related directly after the "Lesser Interpolation" (4:31–6:11), indicating that it is the twelve who accompany Jesus as he travels across the countryside preaching his radical message. However, because of the Luke's particular use of *mathētas*, *dōdeka* and *apostolous*, such an assumption cannot be made. Jesus "names" (*ōnamasen*) the twelve as "apostles." In Mark, the twelve are sent out and return as the apostles; they are not "named" as such. Matthew refers to the "twelve apostles" (*dōdeka apostolon*) only once, in the commissioning pericope (10:2); afterward they are always referred to as the "twelve disciples" (*dōdeka mathētai*). Furthermore, they are not named "apostles," but are given nicknames. This difference, while subtle, intimates that in Luke the "twelve apostles" are a group distinct from the "disciples."

Another feature of the calling of the twelve in Luke is that Judas, for the first and only time in the NT, is referred to as a "traitor" (*prodotēs*). Upon introduction, he is not described as the one who "hands over" (*paradidōmi*) Jesus. As with Matthew's gospel, a change in Peter's character results in a change in Judas'; the two are linked inextricably. We must ask, are Peter and Judas meant to be understood as contrasting models of discipleship? If so, what makes Judas a "traitor"? Likewise, does Peter's role in Jesus' ministry change in any real way, thereby giving him special significance and authority meant to contrast with the perfidiousness of Judas?

The contrast between Peter and Judas in Luke is highly nuanced and complicated, involving two central motifs: (a) how discipleship was understood in the Lukan community; and (b) the role of Satan. The motifs intersect in various narratives, but for now must be treated separately.

First, we must understand the role of discipleship in the Lukan community. Luke retains the traditional language that both Mark and Matthew used to describe the sending out of the twelve (Lk 9:1–6//Mk 6:7–13//Mt 10:1, 9–4): they are to carry no knapsack, no bread, no money and only one shirt, and so on. The mission is to be fraught with peril and adversity (Lk 9:23–7//Mk 8:34–9:1//Mt 16:24–8). There is an important difference in Luke's narrative, however. Unlike Mark, who highlights the denseness of the twelve throughout the gospel, and unlike Matthew, who softens the condemnations by elevating the role of Peter, Luke groups a series of unflattering pericopes regarding the twelve within one chapter, Luke 9 (see vv.29–37, 43–5 and 46–50). None of these narratives is original to Luke, but it is interesting that they are grouped together. Why does Luke do this?

The seventy-two

I believe the answer comes in Lk 10:1–12 (quoted below, with my italics). Here a uniquely Lukan motif is revealed: the existence of "seventy-two others" (*eterous ebdomēkonta*) who are sent out in pairs and given authority.

(1) After this the Lord appointed seventy-two others and sent them on ahead of him in pairs to every town and place that he himself intended to visit. (2) He would say to them, "*Although the crop is good, still there are few to harvest it. So beg the harvest boss to dispatch workers into the fields. (3) Get going; look, I'm sending you out like lambs into a pack of wolves. (4) Carry no purse, no knapsack, no sandals. Don't greet anyone on the road. (5) Whenever you enter a house, first say, "Peace to this house." (6) If peaceful people live there, your peace will rest on them. But if not, it will return to you. (7) Stay at one house, eating and drinking whatever they provide, for workers deserve their*

wages. Do not move from house to house. (8) *Whenever you enter a town and they welcome you, eat whatever is set before you.* (9) *Cure the sick there and tell them, "God's Imperial rule is closing in."* (10) *But whenever you enter a town and they do not receive you, go out into the streets and say,* (11) *"Even the dust of your town that sticks to our feet, we wipe off against you. But know this: God's imperial rule is closing in."* (12) *I tell you, on that say Sodom will be better off than that town.*

What is of particular interest to our investigation is Luke's use of verses from Q – concerning how one is to be a follower of Jesus – to describe the role of the seventy-two. In fact, every verse comes from Q![5]

Unlike Matthew, who emphasizes the twelve, Luke speaks of an entirely new group: the seventy-two are given authority to heal and cast out demons, are told what to carry and what not to carry, and the rest.[6] What does this change indicate? I find the alterations to be evidence that the Lukan community was much larger than either the Markan or the Matthean communities. (It certainly was larger than the Q community.) It is likely that a great number of people were active in the Lukan community, and they were esteemed greatly. However, like the Matthean community, the Lukan community was concerned with rightful authority. If Jesus gave authority only to the twelve, from where would so many people living nearly two generations after Jesus derive their authority? By increasing the number of people who received authority directly from Jesus, the Lukan community could justify its large, active and authoritative ministry. We also might interpret the seventy-two as implicitly including gentiles. The significance of the twelve most certainly is Jewish, referring to the twelve tribes of Israel. Were the seventy-two the gentile equivalent of the twelve, and if so, is the authority of the twelve changed in any way by this group?

I find that the authority of the twelve is changed, although not diminished, in Luke–Acts. While an analysis is difficult in light of the particular use of the terms disciples, apostles and twelve found in 6:13–16,[7] the twelve are still a primary and respected group. Several factors lead me to this position. Special-L material places the twelve close to Jesus (8:1–3). Luke retains the Markan passages concerning the twelve with little or no change (Lk 9:1–6; 9:18–22, 22:31–4, etc.).

When Luke does make changes to Mark's narrative, members of the twelve are highlighted. For example, in Lk 22:7–13 Peter and John are sent by Jesus to make preparations for the Passover; in Mark 14:13, two unnamed disciples are sent; in Matthew 14:17–19, the disciples as an undifferentiated group perform the preparations. While Luke highlights two members of the twelve rather than the whole group, this change makes sense: if there are eighty-four people (before the death of Judas) with authority, singling out two exemplary disciples rather than the "twelve" is logical. The Risen One appears to two of the "eleven" (their number after the death of Judas) on the road (Lk 24:13–27); it is reported that the Risen One has appeared to Simon (Lk 24:34), and He appears to the eleven as a whole in Lk 24:36–53.

In Mark, the twelve never accept the truth about Jesus – that he must be arrested, suffer, die and be raised on the third day. In Luke, the eleven accept this after seeing him resurrected and, though it takes them a while, they come into a fullness of faith. Furthermore, Jesus regards it as so important that the eleven be his emissaries that he grants them a post-resurrection visit to bolster their faith. Jesus giving the eleven/twelve such importance in Mark is unthinkable. The twelve (their number is restored to fullness in Acts 1) are provided with unique authority in Luke: their minds are prepared by Jesus to receive a proper understanding of how the scriptures were fulfilled by the Jesus event (Lk 24:45–8). As I noted above, Luke's gospel establishes Jesus as the Lord of the resurrection; the job of the twelve to evangelize the world is tied to this resurrection. Once again, such an authority is unthinkable in Mark's gospel.

SATAN: A HISTORY

It is difficult to discuss Satan today because there have been centuries of hermeneutics and traditions resting upon a red, horned demon with a bifurcated tail carrying a pitchfork.[8] The word *satan* properly means "adversary." For example, in the Hebrew Bible a *satan* never appears as a character; rather, a *satan* (from the Hebrew root *stn*) is a force or super-natural being sent by God to interrupt human activity.[9] The effects of this intervention either could be good or bad. What is important, however, is that "Satan" as a proper name and a specific character is unknown to the Hebrew Bible and reflects theological developments outside the scriptures. Similarly, the Greek word *diablos*, commonly translated as "devil," means "one who throws something across the path of another." In Hebrew writings, including those found in the Hebrew Bible, the *diablos* was frequently depicted as the prosecuting angel in the heavenly court – again, not a distinct being, but a role to be filled.[10]

In the first-century world, some believed there was a cosmic battle between the forces of good and the forces of evil, and that in fact *satan* was, in a manner of speaking, a proper being. The foremost example is the Essenes, a heavily dualist group that regarded itself as the "Sons of

Light" locked in an eternal battle with the "Sons of Darkness," who were understood to be both fellow Jews who lived in apostasy (first under the leadership of the Hasmoneans and then under the Romans) and those outside the Jewish faith, "the nations" (in Hebrew, *ha goyim*).[11] According to the Essenes' central text, *The Scroll of the War of the Sons of Light Against the Sons of Darkness*, discovered amongst the Dead Sea Scrolls in 1947, God had given them a "Prince of Light" who was their supernatural champion. He helped them in the battle with the "Sons of Darkness" who were under the leadership of Mastema (alternatively called Beliar), the "Prince of Darkness." Those who fell under the sway of *satan* were "traitors."[12]

It is clear from the writings of the Essenes that they regarded the "Prince of Light" as a supernatural force or entity that helped them fight the corresponding evil forces. The ultimate battle went on within the individual person's heart:

> The spirits of truth and falsehood struggle within the human heart . . . According to his share in truth and right, thus a man hates lies, and according to his share in the lot of deceit, thus he hates truth (1 Q Source 4:12–14).[13]

The stakes were high for the Essene community; they removed themselves from society leading a cloistered, regimented life. Though they were apocalyptic, and perhaps influenced by the ancient Persian religion of Zoroastrianism, the Essenes understood themselves to be the rightful inheritors of God's promises, the True Israel. Their beliefs in a cosmic battle between good and evil focused on the individual and his/her role in God's community, not a Revelation-like cosmic war.

SATAN IN LUKE

The Essenes can teach us something about the Lukan community. While we must be careful not to draw parallels unsubstantiated by the evidence, we have already noted that the Lukan community understood itself to be the True Israel, the rightful inheritors of God's love and ancient promises. According to Luke, if you reject Jesus, you reject God; if you reject God, you accept *satan*. The Essenes defined as traitors those who did not practice their brand of Judaism, those who had fallen under the spell of *satan*. Our present task, then, is to ask if the presence of *satan* in Luke's gospel can be used to explain why Judas is referred to as a "traitor" (*prodotēs*).

In Mk 1:12–13, Jesus' testing in the wilderness is related in a per-functory, truncated fashion: "And right away the spirit drives him out into the wilderness, where he remained for forty days, being put to the test by Satan [*tou Satana*]. While he was living there among the wild animals, the heavenly messengers looked after him." *Satan* need not be understood as a person: the forces of evil tempt Jesus, but the forces of good come to his aid. Matthew and Luke (Lk 4:1–13//Mt 4:1–11), using Q, relate a much more elaborate testing of Jesus by the devil (*tou diabo-lou*).[14] In this shared narrative, Jesus is tempted three times: he is asked to turn a stone into bread as proof that he is the Son of God; he is promised total authority over earth if he will pay homage to the devil; and he is asked to jump off a high pinnacle, which would result not in his death, but in heavenly messengers saving him from a gruesome fall. Responding to the first two temptations, Jesus rebukes the devil by citing scripture; with the third temptation, the devil uses Jesus' own method: he quotes Psalm 91:11–12. The method is employed to no avail; Jesus wins the scriptural battle, frustrating the devil's efforts.

Matthew's and Luke's accounts of the temptations are nearly identi-cal, save for two interesting details. First, in Mt 4:11, the devil leaves Jesus – *(h)o diablos apestē apo autou achri kairou* – and does not return; it is implied that Jesus has defeated the devil. However, in Luke, the devil removes himself until another time: *(h)o diablos apestē apo autou achri kairou*. Jesus does not defeat the devil in the desert; rather, for the time being he stymies him. Second, in Mark and Matthew, Jesus is tended to by "angels" (*angeloi*) after his encounter with *satan*/the devil. In Luke, no such agents appear. Jesus is armed with the words of God and nothing else. I find this to be a significant detail: Jesus himself, according to the Lukan community, is the force of good and needs no help from heaven to confront the devil.

When we understand the meaning of *satan* and *diablos*, and the way they are used in Luke–Acts, it is easy to see how the role of the adversary is filled in Luke's gospel: the "chief priests and the Pharisees," who look "to find some excuse to denounce him" (Lk 6:7), stand in direct opposition to Jesus. These individuals are not in collusion with a walking, talking goat-man who embodies evil; rather, it is they who seek to throw an obstacle across Jesus' path: the hierarchs are both *satan* and *diablos*. Jesus, as an embodiment of pure good, is locked in a battle of spiritual warfare with those who oppose him, people the Lukan community understand as submitting to the powers of evil.

Lk 12:51–3 as a test case: *satan* and Jesus in conflict

The eternal battle between good and evil is a central theme in the Lukan Jesus' ministry:

> (51) Do you suppose I came here to bring peace on earth? No, I tell you, on the contrary: conflict. (52) As a result, from now on in any given house there will be five in conflict, three against two and two against three. (53) Father will be pitted against son and son against father, mother against daughter and daughter against mother, mother-in-law against daughter-in-law and daughter-in-law against mother-in-law.

Lines are being drawn and sides taken; the choice as to where one places allegiance is extremely important. The forces that oppose Jesus and those who support him can affect anyone, even one's closest relatives. While this passage originates within the Q community, it is centrally relevant to both Matthew (10:34–6) and Luke, who understand the agents of adversity differently.[15]

Lk 13:31–2 as a test case: Herod and *satan*

Evil is not just an unseen force against which one must be constantly on guard. On the contrary, the writer of Luke–Act warns, the forces that seek to be an adversary (*satan*) to Jesus have found earthly representatives:

> (31) About that time some Pharisees approached and warned him, "Get out of here! Herod wants to kill you." (32) He replied to them, "Go tell that fox, 'Look here, today and tomorrow I'll be driving out demons and healing people, and on the third day I'll be finished'."

While there are many who stand against Jesus in Luke's gospel, he has two primary enemies: Herod and Judas. Let us first examine how *satan* functions in the former. The Pharisees, the primary enemy of Jesus in Matthew's gospel, warn Jesus that Herod is seeking to kill him. Jesus' response in v.32 intimates that Herod's opposition to him is the result of a choice: Herod wishes to be an adversary to Jesus, and is therefore a *satan*.

Lk 10:18–20 as a test case: the seventy-two fight *satan*

Jesus' entire ministry, according to Luke, involves fighting *satan*. In Lk 10:17, the seventy-two, after returning from their mission, report to Jesus that they have been successful in casting out demons. In vv.18–20, Jesus portends *satan*'s ultimate defeat.

> (18) "I was watching Satan fall like lightning from heaven. (19) Look, I have given you authority to step on snakes and scorpions, and over all the power of the enemy; and nothing will ever harm you. (20) However, don't rejoice that the spirits submit to you; rejoice instead that your names have been inscribed in heaven."

It is significant that Jesus empowers the seventy-two with the ability to contribute to *satan*'s defeat, resulting in their gaining access to heaven. To the Lukan community, being a follower of Jesus has earthly and heavenly consequences.[16] *Satan*'s presence in Mark and Matthew is not so pronounced because, unlike Luke, their christologies and soteriologies do not revolve around God's ultimate defeat of evil.

By now it should be apparent that the Lukan community understood Jesus' ministry to be the culmination of God's cosmic battle with *satan*, the force or entity that opposes good. According to the Lukan community, there were dire consequences for choosing the wrong side. One is a proper follower of Jesus by fighting against *satan*. How does this, then, relate to our discussion of Judas?

"Then Satan took possession of Judas, the one called Iscariot"

After the tempting in the desert, the *satan* removes himself until a more opportune time arises. Though Herod and certain Pharisees work against Jesus, there is no explicit mention of a *satan* influencing them. Such is not the case with Judas. Lk 22:3–6 reads:

> (3) Then Satan took possession of Judas, the one called Iscariot, who was a member of the twelve. (4) He went off to negotiate with the ranking priests and officers on a way to turn Jesus over to them. (5) They were delighted, and consented to pay him silver. (6) And Judas accepted the deal, and began looking around for the right moment to turn him over to them when a crowd was not around.

Important differences arise between the Markan and Matthean accounts of Judas' role in the death of Jesus and that offered in Luke. First, Judas is possessed by *satan*. The cosmic battle begun in the desert has resumed. Judas acts in collusion with the ranking priests and officers, whom Luke has already established as adversaries to Jesus; and therefore, under the influence of *satan*, Judas becomes the primary figure through whom *satan* is able to act. Second, Judas does not resist the offer for money, part of *satan*'s second temptation of Jesus. Judas' poor choice is contrasted with the wholly right choice made by Jesus. Third, Luke does not state the amount of money Judas is paid. The Matthean detail of thirty silver pieces, possibly alluding to Jesus being purchased for the price of a slave, is not repeated; therefore, the impact upon the listener/reader is different. Judas acts purely out of greed; his choice has been made and, we can safely assume, he has chosen poorly.

In Lk 22:31, *satan* is mentioned again:

> Simon, Simon, look out, Satan is after all of you, to winnow you like wheat. But I have prayed for you that your trust may not give out. And once you have recovered, you are to shore up these brothers of yours [*tous adelphous sou*].[17]

The listener/reader already knows that Judas has been possessed, but, according to Jesus, Judas is not the only one in danger: Simon could falter as well. This passage is used to set up Peter's promise to remain faithful to Jesus, an oath we have seen in both Mark and Luke.[18] However, Luke adds an important detail: though Simon will falter, it is explicitly stated that he will recover and take a leading role in the community. As I noted above, Peter's authority is recognized by the Lukan community, and his denial is not regarded as an impediment to the authenticity of that authority. This addition causes the listener/reader to contrast Peter's action of denying Jesus, and his subsequent recovery, with the actions of Judas, the one called "traitor."

Other than being possessed by *satan*, the Lukan Judas performs the same actions as reported in Mark and Matthew. He hands over (*paradidōmi*) Jesus to the authorities, which in itself is not a traitorous act; he receives money for his action, but no specific amount is mentioned. Again, being a paid informant was an accepted part of both Roman and Jewish society. Why, then, does Luke call Judas a traitor (*prodotēs*)? Because of his possession by *satan* and only because of his possession by *satan*. Considering the evidence, no other conclusion can be drawn.

The Lukan community is being admonished to be constantly vigilant; even a member of Jesus' inner circle, Judas, gave in to temptation and chose to become an adversary. Judas decided to set himself up against the ideal of good, and in this way himself became evil. Jesus knew that any one of his followers could be led astray by the evil forces, and he warned them against choosing to become adversaries. The message is clear: every follower of Jesus has the potential to become an adversary; only by remaining true to the principles of good can one be saved. In my estimation, Luke's gospel provides us with the only narrative in which Judas Iscariot is presented as the archetype of improper discipleship. He is a traitor because he chose to become a *satan*, and not to remain a follower of Jesus.

THE DEATH OF JUDAS ISCARIOT IN LUKE–ACTS

(15) In those days Peter stood up among the believers (together the crowd numbered one hundred twenty persons) and said, (16) "Friends, the scripture had to be fulfilled, which the Holy Spirit through David foretold concerning Judas, who became a guide for those who arrested Jesus— (17) for he was numbered among us and was allotted his share in this ministry." (18) (Now this man acquired a field with the reward of his wickedness; and falling headlong, he burst open in the middle and all his bowels gushed out. (19) This became known to all the residents in Jerusalem, so that the field was called in their language Hakeldama, that is, Field of Blood.) (20) "For it is written in the book of Psalms, 'Let his homestead become desolate, and let there be no one to live in it'; and 'Let another take his position of overseer.' (21) So one of the men who have accompanied us, from the time that the Lord Jesus went in and out among us, (22) beginning from the baptism of John until the day he was taken up from us—one of these must become a witness with us to his resurrection." (23) So they proposed two . . . (26) And they cast lots for them, and the lot fell on Matthias; and he was added to the eleven apostles.

That Judas' death is related in Acts 1:15–26 is significant, for Acts is concerned with the formation of the Church. The twelve play a central role in establishing the rightful *ekklesia*; not surprisingly, Peter is the one who addresses those assembled and leads the search for a new member of the twelve. In order for God's plans for the True Israel to continue, a representative of each tribe must be present and must have seen the Risen One.

The death of Judas Iscariot must be explained as well. His demise in

Acts is difficult to unpack, because there are thematic inconsistencies. Peter, in his address, makes no mention of *satan*, which, as we have already discussed, is central to Luke's depiction of Judas. Peter refers to Judas as he "who became a guide for those who arrested Jesus" (*tou genomenou odēgou tois sullabousin Iēsoun*). There is no reference to the "handing over" (*paradidōmi*) of Jesus; if we had only this passage from Acts, it would be difficult to understand why Judas deserved such a brutal death.

There are noticeable differences between Matthew's account and that found in Acts:

1   Judas himself purchases the field with the money he received from his "wickedness" (*adikia*), instead of the priests buying the field with the blood money.
2   Acts provides a different account for why the field is called the "Field of Blood"; the blood spilled belongs to Judas, and no mention is made of the money used to purchase it.
3   According to Acts, the field is called the "Field of Blood" in Aramaic; Matthew does not include this detail.
4   Luke notes that the field is well known near Jerusalem, a detail missing in Matthew.
5   Matthew describes the field as a burial place for foreigners, Acts implies that Judas made his home there.
6   Matthew is specific about the length of time it takes Jesus to die, whereas no time-frame is offered in Luke's account.
7   Different Hebrew prophecies are supposedly fulfilled by the event in Matthew and Acts. In Acts 1:20, two separate psalms are cited: Ps 69:25 and Ps 109:8 (which is changed in the Acts texts; the proper translation is "May his days be few; may another seize his position").[19]
8   Judas' place must be filled in Acts; Matthew does not show this concern.
9   The manner of death is much different; in Matthew, Judas hangs himself; in Acts, Judas dies by a headlong fall (or, as it is sometimes translated, by being burst apart).
10 Judas displays contrition in Matthew's gospel, but does not do so in Acts.

As I noted in Chapter 5, folklore is rarely uniform. The above differences bring into question the historicity of both narratives. However, similarities between the two accounts must also be taken into consideration:

1   Both accounts connect the purchasing of the field to the money Judas receives for his role in Jesus' arrest.

2   Both accounts provide a similar name for the field, although Matthew refers to it as *agros aimatos* ("Field of Blood" or "Bloody Field"), whereas Acts terms it *chorion aimatos* (properly, an "Acre of Blood").

3   Both place the field in a named location, presumably known, though the locations differ.

4   Both claim that Scripture was fulfilled through the Judas event.

5   Both accounts provide a death narrative.

6   Both appear to draw on popular traditions.

The discrepancies far outweigh the similarities; furthermore, the two accounts have different objectives. Luke's primary concern in Acts 1:15–26 is to provide legitimacy and continuity for the twelve; more verses are dedicated to the election of Matthias (six) than to the figure of Judas (five). Judas is secondary, a nuisance that must be dealt with; no interest is shown in his feelings regarding the death of Jesus. On the other hand, Matthew's account has no connection to the twelve, and Judas' death is an act of contrition; he displays remorse for his action and, by taking his own life, makes a definitive statement about his regret.

One cannot regard the death account in Matthew as historical and then disregard the account in Acts, or vice versa, for there exists no outside source that can substantiate the veracity of one or the other. In fact it is impossible to regard either as historical, even when we take into consideration the shared details. If we assume that Judas is an historical figure, how does he die? The two accounts give different answers. If the "Field of Blood" is historical, where is it? Both provide different locations. For what purpose is the field used? Matthew claims it is the burial place for foreigners, and is well known in his time; Acts says it remains desolate, so no one could be buried there. Since even the "shared" details have no harmony, it is abundantly clear that Judas' death, like his life, is fictional.

Die like Jesus

If Judas' life and death are fictitious, as I have contended, what purpose does he play in Luke–Acts? As I have argued above, Judas emerges as the prototype for improper discipleship in Luke's gospel. His death also teaches followers of Jesus that if they choose *satan* – that is, become an adversary – God will strike them down.

Judas' death in Acts is described in Greek as *prēnēs genomēnos*, commonly translated as "falling forward." This type of death is also described in Wis 4:19, where the godless meet a similar fate as Judas:

> In death their bodies will be dishonored, and among the dead they will be the object of contempt for ever; he shall strike them speechless, fling them headlong (*preneis*), shake them from their foundations, and make a desert of them; they shall be full of anguish, and all memory of them shall perish.[20]

God strikes down those who reject him, flinging them headlong into the abyss. I argue that Judas does not take his own life in Acts, because voluntary death can be understood as honorable, or at the very least, a sign of contrition for one's life. Rather, in Acts, the villainous Judas chooses to become an adversary to good and suffers the ultimate consequence, a brutal death at the hand of God. Once again, good triumphs over evil, a central message of Luke's gospel. The message is clear: God always wins, and *satan*'s minions never escape unscathed.

Intra-textual evidence in Acts indicates that the standards of discipleship for the Lukan community include a proper death. The ministry and martyrdom of Stephen is related in Acts 6:8–8:la. Like Jesus, Stephen preaches against the Temple and adjures the people to change their stiff-necked ways. Like Jesus, Stephen is charged and sentenced to death. Like Jesus, Stephen asks for his persecutors to be forgiven. Like Jesus, Stephen asks the Lord to receive his spirit. Like Jesus, Stephen lives an honorable life and dies an honorable death, one that results in his spirit being received by the Lord. Like Jesus, Stephen dies a martyr. Acts 6:8–8:la is midrash (commentary) on how one is a proper follower of Jesus.

Acts 5:1–11, on the other hand, is midrash on how one is not a follower of Jesus. Ananias and Sapphira, married followers of Jesus, sell some property and do not give the appropriate amount to the apostles. Learning of this, Peter questions the husband. " 'Ananias,' Peter asked, 'Why has Satan filled your heart to lie to the Holy Spirit and to keep back part of the proceeds of the land? . . . You have not lied to us, but to God!' Now when Ananias heard these words, he fell down [*pesōn*] and died." (vv.3, 4b–5a). In vv.7–10, Peter questions Sapphira as to whether she was aware of her husband's actions. When she answers in the affirmative, Peter says to her: " 'How is it that you have agreed together to put the Spirit of the Lord to the test? Look, the feet of those who have buried your husband are at the door, and they will carry you out.' Immediately she fell down [*pesōn*] at his feet and died." The couple's improper actions are the result of collusion with Satan, just as Judas' actions were, and the result is death at the hand of God, just like Judas. The message is clear: those who choose Satan will experience immediate deaths bereft of honor.

Evidence outside the New Testament indicates that proper disciple-ship was understood to entail the death of a martyr. Ignatius of Antioch, an early bishop (literally, "overseer") of the Church, wrote a letter to the Christian community in Rome c. 110 CE. In this letter, he states that he will become a disciple of the Anointed through a martyr's death; he is so assured of this eventuality that he begs his fellow believers not to take any action that might prevent him from this death. He writes:

> I am corresponding with all the churches and bidding them all realize that I am voluntarily dying for God—if, that is, you do not interfere. I plead with you, do not do me an unseasonable kindness. Let me be fodder for wild beasts—that is how I can get to God. I am God's pure wheat and I am being ground by the teeth of wild beasts to make a pure loaf for Christ. I would rather you fawn on the beasts so that they may be my tomb and no scrap of my body left. Thus, when I have fallen asleep, I shall be a burden no more. Then I shall be a real disciple of Jesus Christ when the world sees my body no more . . . I shall coax them on to eat me up at once and not to hold off, as sometimes happens, through fear. And if they are reluctant, I shall force them to it. Forgive me—I know what is good to me. Now is the moment I am beginning to be a disciple.[21]

Ignatius received his wish: he died a martyr's death. His belief that one is a proper follower of Jesus by dying like Jesus was not idiosyncratic; in fact, by the third century, many Church leaders were concerned that Christianity was becoming a death cult. Too many people thought they could be Christians by dying at the hands of the oppressors.

CONCLUSIONS

In Luke–Acts, and for the only time in the Christian scriptures, Judas is called a "traitor." From the evidence available to us, Judas' traitorous act consists of choosing to be an adversary to good by siding with *satan* over Jesus. As a result of his choice, Judas is struck down by God. The narrative seems logical, in light of the reality of the Luke–Acts com-munity: faced with persecution that invariably results in death, the standards of discipleship are changed to include a proper death. One is to die like Jesus/Stephen, not like Judas/Ananias and Sapphira. When one dies a martyr's death, one goes to God; when one allies with *satan*, one is struck down.

There is no evidence that the death narrative of Judas Iscariot found in Acts 1:15–26 is historical, nor does it need to be. The Lukan community is concerned with the structure of the Church, which ultimately explains why Judas' death account is included in the gospel; thus the presence of Matthias can be explained. Luke is unable to escape the figure of Judas introduced in Mark, so, like Matthew, Luke changes Judas to fit the christology and theology of the community.

By recasting the history of Israel in terms of the Jesus event, Luke, in many ways, recasts the history of Christianity. Judas becomes the symbol for *satan*. The consequence, unfortunately, is that the Jews themselves are associated with *satan*, and it becomes more and more common to regard Judas as the representative of the Jews. What also emerges, however, is the idea that voluntary death is the tool of Satan. This is peculiar because, in Luke–Acts, Judas does not commit suicide. However, when the New Testament canon was formed, the need for biblical harmony was born. The result was the version of Judas' death contained in a letter by the seventh-century Christian Theophylact:

> [Judas] put his neck into the halter and hanged himself on a certain tree, but the tree bent down and he continued to live, since it was God's will that he either be preserved for repentance or public disgrace, and shame. For they say that due to dropsy he could not pass where a wagon passed with ease; then he fell on his face and burst asunder, that is, was rent apart, as Luke says in Acts.[22]

Details hitherto unrelated are now joined together, with non-biblical folklore mixed in. Emerging is a picture of Judas Iscariot as an historical figure that can be found nowhere in the Bible. Over the centuries, Judas' suicide became anathema to Christians because the common view of Judas Iscariot combined all the most discreditable elements about him in the scriptures. In fact, they do not. With the attempt to harmonize widely different interpretations of Jesus and Judas began the many deaths of Judas Iscariot.

Part III

Resurrection?

7   Conclusions

"They always dick around with it, you know?" he says. "Judas is always some kind of friend of some freedom fighter named Barabbas, you know what I mean? It is horseshit. It's revisionist horseshit. And that's what those academics are into . . . Just get an academic on board if you want to pervert something."

Mel Gibson[1]

When the gospels are regarded as unbiased, factual accounts of history, dangerous things happen: Jews are murdered as "Christ-killers"; homosexuals are strapped to fence posts and left to die for violating God's "divine will"; and people who voluntarily die are regarded as betrayers of God. The Bible is used to justify this behavior and, as a newly baptized Christian, I am already tired of it. I have written this book in hopes of somehow contributing to a better understanding of Judas Iscariot and how his voluntary death might have been understood historically.

I put forth some bold theories in this book. I firmly believe that Judas Iscariot is not an historical figure; as a result, it is possible that I engage in "revisionist horseshit." I do not ask that the reader believe everything I have put forth. It is enough that the book is read and Judas is discussed. For those of us who have loved ones who killed themselves, too often the figure of Judas Iscariot is presented as an example of a suicide who is in hell. The message to us is clear: As goes Judas, so goes your loved one. But this view can be found nowhere in the Bible; nowhere in the gospels or the epistles of Paul is there anything to indicate that such is the case. But everyday this viewpoint is spit from vitriolic lips, and as a result people are hurt and damaged.

What we know about Judas

Let us look at what we can establish. When we pull the gospel narratives apart and attempt to determine everything we "know" about Judas, we are left with surprisingly little: Judas was a member of the twelve, though, as I have pointed out, we should be skeptical of this report because it is made first by Mark, who has a clear agenda against the twelve. Throughout the Gospel of Mark, members of the twelve are portrayed as bumbling Keystone cops who consistently and constantly miss the point of Jesus' ministry. Mark's gospel represents the first time Judas Iscariot appears in writings about Jesus of Nazareth, and there is a deliberate attempt to connect Judas to the twelve: he is always introduced as "Judas Iscariot, one of the twelve." To paraphrase the Bard, methinks the author of Mark doth protest too much. As I argued in Chapter 3, by the time Judas appears to hand Jesus over to the authorities, the collective character of this group has already been besmirched by Peter, John, James and Andrew. The listener/reader has lost all confidence in the twelve, and understands that they represent the paradigm for improper discipleship.

What else can we know about Judas? From the scant information provided in Mark's gospel, we can surmise that Judas did nothing of exceptional merit or detriment during his life. His successes were the successes of the twelve; his failures were the failures of the twelve. What we do know, however, is that Judas decided to "hand over" Jesus to the authorities. To claim his act was a betrayal is fallacious. The Greek verb *paradidōmi* properly means "to hand over." Nowhere in extant Greek literature is the verb translated as "betray." The idea that Judas "betrayed" Jesus is the result of later Christian hermeneutics and homiletics (and the subject of my next book). We do not know Judas' motives.

According to Mark, Judas was paid silver, but we do not know how much. Matthew elaborates upon this detail and informs the listener/reader that Judas was paid the sum of thirty silver pieces. According to Jewish law, thirty pieces was the amount paid for a slave. It is possible that the payment of thirty silver pieces to Judas was meant to be symbolic: Jesus was purchased for the price of a slave, and through his redemptive death saved all humanity from being enslaved by sin and death. However, it is unclear if such was Matthew's intention. What is clear, however, is that Judas gave the money back, throwing it into the Temple and declaring Jesus to be "innocent blood." According to my reading, this was one of three acts of contrition performed by Judas in Matthew's gospel. In Luke–Acts, however, the story is different. Judas is paid "in silver" according to Luke 22:5, but no specific amount is mentioned.

Both Matthew and Luke mention that an area of land was purchased with the money, but their accounts differ greatly in the details. According to Matthew, the priests purchased a potter's field near Jerusalem with blood money; as a result, the land was known as the Field of Blood. This event was connected to a prophecy in Jeremiah. According to Acts 1, Judas purchased a field near Jerusalem, where he was struck down by God for his wickedness, resulting in the land being widely known as *Akel'dama*, Aramaic for Field of Blood. This detail was connected to a prophecy in Psalms. The accounts do not agree on the location of the field, the events leading to the purchase of the field, or the specific Hebrew prophecies portending the actions of Judas. In reality, we do not know much about Judas Iscariot at all.

We can know one thing, however: if Judas lived, he had to die. But how his death occurred is problematic. Mark does not discuss the death of Judas. According to Matthew, who wrote sometime between 80 and 85 CE, Judas took his own life: he died as a result of hanging. It seems clear that Judas' death was his own choice. Overcome by anguish and regret at "handing over" Jesus, Judas ended his own life. I can find nothing in the Hebrew Bible or Jewish oral law – or even a philosophy prevalent at the time Judas lived – to suggest that the taking of one's own life was considered a sin. Certainly, there were those who regarded voluntary death as undesirable, even unethical or immoral. But it also was believed that taking one's own life could lead to a noble death if one received the *anangke*, a sign indicating that death was a necessity and required by the gods (God). Furthermore, according to ancient beliefs, voluntary death could be an act of contrition. There is no evidence to suggest that one system of thought was more common or accepted than another; people were divided then just as we are divided now. Considering Matthew's narrative, I believe Judas' own death was the result of great personal anguish and the desire to set things right between himself and God. It seems clear to me the members of Matthew's community understood Judas' death in this light.

An entirely different death is recounted in Acts 1. Judas has allied himself with *satan*. I have argued that *satan* should not be understood as a red-skinned demon with a bifurcated tail who carries a pitchfork. Rather, *satan* is an adversary, one who seeks to be a stumbling block to the forces of good. The Lukan Judas, for whatever reasons, decides to set himself up against Jesus, the embodiment of pure good. In this way, Judas sides with evil and becomes a traitor (*prodotēs*) to Jesus. After successfully handing Jesus over, Judas decides to take his earnings and purchase a field. God strikes Judas down, clearly demonstrating to the listener/reader that in the cataclysmic battle between good and evil, good will always triumph. A similar story is told in Acts 5:1–11, when Ananias and Sapphira are struck down by God for not tithing to the Roman Church. Their dishonorable deaths are juxtaposed with the honorable death of Stephen the martyr, just as Judas' dishonorable death is juxtaposed with Jesus' honorable and salvific death on the cross. The message in Luke–Acts is much different: one should die like Jesus and Stephen, performing the will of God, and not like Judas and Ananias and Sapphira, who chose to be adversaries to the forces of good.

What if Judas had never existed?

Whether or not Judas Iscariot existed, ultimately, is not important to me. What is important is how he has been used in the Christian tradition. Nowhere in the scriptures is a voluntary death commented upon as a negative act. Furthermore, only once in all the New Testament is Judas actually called a "traitor" (*prodotēs*), and it comes in Luke–Acts, where Judas is struck down by God for being aligned with Satan. If Judas did betray God, it was not because of his death but as a result of a choice he made in his life. Simply put: voluntary death is not a sin.

A fine line has always been drawn between martyrdom and "suicide," when there is very little difference between the two. Ignatius of Antioch and the victims of the 11 September 2001 attacks who jumped to their deaths rather than die of smoke inhalation all made a choice to die in a way that seemed congruous with their lives and their desires. Most Christians revere the martyrs, many of whom are saints, and most compassionate people would have a difficult time saying that any victim of the September 11th attacks betrayed God, no matter how they died. My brother, on the other hand, is seen by many as a "Judas," one who took control out of God's hands and made himself godlike, thereby betraying the divine, when, in fact, Stephen also made a choice that was congruous with his life and his reality. I have no doubt that Stephen received the divine *anangke*. I can never know if this is true, but those who revile "suicides" cannot know, either. No one was there when Stephen died. And those of us in the Judeo-Christian tradition must accept that God's grace is not something we can quantify and qualify, not something we can limit with arbitrary parameters. The Bible does not say that God abhors voluntary death; for Christians, the New Testament seems to support voluntary death under certain circumstances, such as the deaths of Jesus and Stephen the martyr. Why is my Stephen any different? What makes his death a sin against God?

I opened this book with a quotation from Augustine, one to which I would like to return.

> For it is clear that, if no one has a private right to kill even a guilty man (and no law allows this), then certainly anyone who kills himself is a murderer, and is the more guilty in killing himself the more innocent he is of the charge on which he has condemned himself to death. We rightly abominate the act of Judas, and the judgment of truth is that when he hanged himself he did not atone for the guilt of his detestable betrayal but rather increased it, since he despaired of God's mercy and in a fit of self-destructive remorse left himself no chance of a saving repentance. How much less right has anyone to indulge in self-slaughter when he can find in himself no fault to justify such a punishment! For when Judas killed himself, he killed a criminal, and yet he ended his life guilty not only of Christ's death, but also of his own; one crime led to another. Why then should a man, who has done no wrong, do wrong to himself? Why should he kill the innocent in putting himself to death, to prevent a guilty man from doing it? Why should he commit a sin against himself to deprive someone else of the chance?

Christians who vilify Judas and people who kill themselves get their information not from the Bible – though they claim to do so – but from thinkers such as Augustine. Certainly, it would be simplistic to attribute negative attitudes toward voluntary death exclusively to Augustine. But such a claim would be anachronistic. Augustine did not voice a unique opinion. At some point in the Christian tradition, voluntary death was regarded as a sin. Perhaps it was a popular belief in Jewish or Near Eastern communities; perhaps it was regarded as obvious that killing oneself was undesirable, so no explicit prohibition was written. While these theories are possible, the simple fact remains that they are not supported by the biblical texts. Other authorities made voluntary death a sin, not the scriptures.

Augustine is wrong throughout the quotation above. In ancient societies there were laws that allowed one to kill oneself, as we discovered in Chapter 4; I find it ironic that Augustine, who so revered Plato, was ignorant of Plato's own criteria for acceptable conditions in which voluntary death could be actualized. While it is unclear if Judas' act of voluntary death is properly "repentance," no system of "Christian" repentance had been forged. We cannot hold Judas to a non-existent standard. Furthermore, Augustine operates under the assumption that Judas had to receive forgiveness from Jesus, not from God. Augustine was not there when Judas hanged himself, so how does Augustine know if God forgave him or not? When Augustine is seen as a greater authority than the Bible, serious problems arise. It is my hope that we can finally rectify the situation here. It is time to let Judas die, once and for all.

What to do with Judas

I have an agenda: my own brother voluntarily ended his life and it is important to me that I defend his honor, that I make a definitive statement attesting to the goodness of his character and the state of his soul. Such a desire does not make me an unbiased observer; I readily admit this fact. But I assemble the evidence, I do not manufacture it. Judas is a problematic figure in the New Testament, and it is unclear to me how he is meant to be interpreted.

Doing away with Judas has consequences. Billions of Christians throughout the two thousand years of religious development and indoctrination have confronted Judas. Some have reviled him; some have defended him; some have not given him much thought. But he is there. His existence or non-existence may be inconsequential to me, but it is not to many Christians, and I must be respectful of that. It is very easy to tear down; it is much harder to build up. Now that I have torn Judas down, what do I offer people as an adequate substitute? This is a question I must address.

I can only understand Judas as an archetype. But the Judas archetype brought me to faith. In the darkest hour of my life, when I sat surrounded by pictures depicting Stephen as a smiling, vibrant man full of promise whose life was cut short by a vicious disease that few people understand, I was at a crossroads. My lifelong desire for faith could have ended on that bitter night, but it did not. In fact, my spiritual life *began* as a result of my brother's death. In this way, Stephen's suicide stands as a testament to the power of God's love and grace. At a time when most people would expect an agnostic to become an atheist, I felt God enter my life. I experienced God putting a stop to my descent into darkness; as I stood on the precipice of the abyss, I did not fall. A deep, surpassing understanding prevented me from cascading into selfish questioning and anger towards God. Instead, I felt the real and life-affirming presence of God as the Loving One. I encountered the God who lifted overwhelming pain and suffering from Stephen and gave it to those who loved him; the God who dispersed Stephen's burden into dozens of little shares and scattered them, like a Diaspora, to his family and friends, who took them happily, knowing that Stephen was finally at peace. This experience was so life-changing and overwhelming, I was baptized by my father-in-law and publicly proclaimed myself a believing Christian. Some may argue with my beliefs; some even try to take the label of Christian away from me because of my thoughts and ideas about God and Jesus, but they cannot take away what God has given freely.

When I confront Judas in the pages of Mark, Matthew and Luke–Acts, I see very real details concerning the human condition. I see eagerness, impatience and poor decisions. I see the parts of myself that prevented me from having the compassion and understanding to love and support Stephen before he was officially diagnosed with schizophrenia. Just as Judas failed to stand by Jesus – which was not a sin but perhaps a testimonial to his loyalty – I failed to stand by Stephen. I had my reasons for this. Stephen said hurtful things. He knew how to reduce me to tears of anger with only a few words; he knew how to manipulate my darkest insecurities and subject them to ridicule. At age 21, I was more concerned with protecting myself from pain than I was with helping my brother confront his demons. I did not have the wherewithal to understand the reality of the situation, so I broke off contact with Stephen. I did not speak to him for a year. In the way some think of Judas, I turned my back on Stephen because he was not what I thought he should be. I was selfish. I held Stephen to unfair standards. In this way, Judas is all of us who have expectations and do not understand that life often requires us to accept and confront that which makes us uncomfortable.

In many ways, Stephen's illness prepared me to love God. Loving someone without needing anything in return is incredibly difficult. But that is what it takes to love a person with a mental illness. Stephen was not capable of having a reciprocal relationship, but that did not mean that he was unworthy or not needing of love. In fact, Stephen needed love more than ever. As his only brother, I saw it as my responsibility to love and support Stephen in any way I could. Although I have regrets – I wish I had done more; I wish I had spoken more openly to him about my feelings and his illness – I did my best. I learned how to love him without needing anything in return, to love him without requesting *quid pro quo*. I learned that I sometimes am a selfish person in regard to love, that I expect others to make things better for me, to make my life better. In truth, love exists without immediate benefit or reward, because love is its own reward. I learned that by loving Stephen unconditionally, without expectation. I loved Stephen because he was deserving of love, because loving him was the right thing to do. When Stephen died, God entered my life. I love God in the same way I loved my sick brother, without expectation or conditions. I love God because loving God is the right thing to do.

I see other things in Judas Iscariot, other difficult truths we all must face. I see that the expectations others have of God can cause misunderstandings. Historically, Christians have expected that God would revile a mortal who had a role to play in the death of the divine son. Theologies and christologies were developed to support this expectation. But it is Christianity that judges Judas, not God. Our understanding of Judas tries to limit God's creative capacity for forgiveness and love. This is troubling to me. Too often there is more judgment than acceptance in Christianity, even when it should be clear that God's love is abundant, alive and here for us to embrace. Perhaps we see in Judas what we do not like about ourselves. Instead of confronting our own shortcomings, we revel in God's supposed judgment of Judas, happy that we can point to someone who, we feel, is far worse than ourselves. But I think that most of us are like Judas. We make mistakes. We feel arrogant and believe that we know what is right and act accordingly. But when we are wrong, we seek forgiveness. We desire restitution. I hope most of us are able to receive it from our fellow human beings in greater doses than we have extended to Judas.

Perhaps there is something more important to learn from Judas, an ultimate lesson about the limits of human nature and the unlimited nature of God. Let us consider a simple fact: most of us lead lives that are misunderstood by others, lives that often are judged by others based upon small bits of information. A mis-step here or an ungraceful comment there can be spread like wildfire within the community, and opinions are formed by those whom we have never met. Condemnations are made, aspersions are cast, and within a short period of time our characters are deemed poor by people who know little or nothing about the situation – and even less about the intricacies and details of our lives, beliefs and deeds. Perhaps what we have done is terrible; horrific even.

But what of this judgment from others? Is it to last the whole of our lives? Is it to follow us around, attached to us like some sort of vindictive scarlet letter? What if, unknown to the casual observers who chose to judge us based on isolated incidents, we set things right with the person or persons we harmed? What if we apologize, humbly seeking forgiveness, displaying deep contrition? What if this forgiveness is granted? Tears are shed, but fences are mended. Love overcomes anger and hatred. Compassion overcomes condemnation. But years down the line, our mis-step or ungraceful comment is remembered by those outside the situation. They continue to condemn us, to judge us. What do we say to those people? Do we attempt to explain the situation? Do we seek to make amends with people whom we never harmed in the first place?

In truth, most Christians judge Judas in this way, based upon an event that they do not fully understand. They act as though Judas harmed them. They condemn him as ungodly, as evil and disgusting. But I see more God in Judas than I do in Peter. I see in Judas the sad face of historic Christianity: while love and acceptance are preached, they are rarely practiced much. Many Christians point the finger and sharply condemn, all the while giving lip service to forgiveness and love. But in the end, it is God who is the source of forgiveness and love, and God extends it without qualification. I know this from personal experience; I have been transformed by this love. I have been forgiven for forsaking my brother. So I believe the story of Judas is a stark reminder that too often we judge based upon very little information. It is never good to be judgmental, but it is especially dangerous when we are on the periphery of a situation; when we condemn others based on limited information, we place our judgment over and against the forgiveness of those directly affected. What did Judas ever do to any of us? Nothing. But the hatred I see for Judas in many Christians' eyes frightens and confounds me. To them I say: do not underestimate the power of God's forgiveness, especially in favor of hatred and judgment.

To those who are unsatisfied with my theology, I have nothing more to offer except questions. If you insist that Judas existed, and you insist that Judas was punished by God and resides in hell for all eternity, what do you gain by this? Does it make you feel better about yourself? Does it help you be a more loving, accepting person who humbly walks the path set for us by Jesus? Does reviling Judas and condemning those who kill themselves add to your spiritual growth and existence? Do you grow closer to God, treat others with amicability and patience, and learn to forgive yourself and others by using Judas as an example of one beyond forgiveness? What does your view of Judas say about God? Is God unable to forgive Judas, or does God choose not to? Are you so much better than Judas that you should revel in the fact that some are beyond forgiveness? Personally, I am not so arrogant that I feel comfortable to judge anyone, even those who judge me and cause me pain and harm. I believe in the transformative power of love and forgiveness, and I learned that from the myth of Judas Iscariot.

IS IT REALLY THAT BAD?

Many might object – and not without adequate reason – that a majority of the world's religions have adopted positions on voluntary death that reflect modern understandings of science, physiology and psychology. Such statements, largely speaking, are true. Although it is difficult to find an "official" stance toward voluntary death, because no such documents exist, a great majority of the world's faith traditions recognize the complexities and subtleties that lead a person to end his or her life. Many people to whom I've spoken – from Buddhists to Muslims – express deep sympathy and care for my brother and my family when I tell them the story of Stephen's life and death.

However, it is overly simplistic to say that a gradual change in attitude displayed by a few equates to a universal change. Indeed, one need only type the phrase "suicide is a sin" into any Internet search engine, and a flood of sites denouncing voluntary death as sinful fill the computer screen. Many of these individuals point to scriptural reference, Church teaching or folk wisdom that is deeply entrenched in society. Without question, there are individual members of the clergy and the laity in all faiths that preach love, understanding and the need to abstain from condemnation, but there are still an overwhelming number of people who hold antiquated ideas about voluntary death. In fact, within the last century there have been sermons delivered from the pulpit condemning suicide. How, then, is it acceptable to say that attitudes have changed? In order to undo centuries of indoctrination and ignorance, more than an intangible, abstract notion of moderated attitudes must be present.

Some disagree with my stance that not enough has been done to change popular beliefs. I have been confronted by some who seem confounded by my statements that people have condemned my brother. One individual told me I was wrong to state my position as strongly as I do, as though I am imagining the ignorance I have confronted throughout my life. My response to this objection? I wish I *were* making it up; then the problem would be of my own doing and therefore chimerical, a much easier situation to resolve.

To illustrate my point that things have not changed, at least not enough to stop the harm perpetrated upon those of us who have lost family members to suicide, I offer one last example. In 1956, less than sixty years ago, the Methodist minister and professor William E. Sangster published a sermon entitled "The traitor who sold Him." I will spare the reader the long litany of objections I have to Sangster's sermon – for most of the objections have already been raised in the preceding chapters – but one passage in particular represents perfectly the popular, pervasive attitude I find so troubling. Note how he uses the words "betrayal" and "betrayed" without comment. Sangster writes:

> Finally, we may learn, I think, from the sad story of Judas, how wrong it is ever to limit our Lord's forgiveness. After the betrayal, Judas took his own life. He forgot his betrayed Master's message of forgiveness. Perhaps he was not listening when Jesus said that the love of God was so mighty that it would always meet penitence with pardon. Perhaps he was wondering whether there was enough in the bag to take a little more!
>
> But knowing what you know of the forgiveness of God, do you think that if Judas had gone, not to hang himself, but to the cross, and flung himself before our dying Lord and said, "Lord Jesus, forgive me"—if he had done that, do you think that Christ who prayed for His murderers as they nailed Him to the wood, and who said to the dying thief, "Today shalt thou be with me in paradise," that that same Savior would have refused forgiveness to the man who kissed Him into their arms?
>
> I cannot believe it. It was the crowning error of Judas' miserable life. Do not add that sin to any others you may have committed. Do not be like the man with whom I wrestled recently to a late hour, who, having reviewed the enormities of his past, denied that God would forgive him, and went out, as Judas went out that night, with the mark of Cain on him and without faith that God would ever wipe it away.
>
> Put no limit to the grace of God![2]

Sangster is first and foremost making a theological statement: Judas compounded his sin by not believing in God's forgiveness; he placed a limit on the grace of God. This is a common position levelled against Judas. I have argued to the contrary: voluntary death was often regarded as the ultimate sign of repentance, displaying a deep sense of contrition and heartfelt remorse.

However, let us argue that Judas' act cannot be interpreted as an act of repentance. How does Sangster, or anyone for that matter, know what was in Judas' heart or mind when he died? Why does Sangster require that Judas seek forgiveness from Jesus, who, at the time, was surrounded by Roman soldiers and wracked by pain and suffering?

Unless I am greatly mistaken, it is not the forgiveness granted by Jesus the human being that concerns Sangster, but rather the forgiveness of Jesus the Divine. To be exculpated, Judas needs a divine pardon. But how can Sangster be certain that Judas did not repent and receive forgiveness from God the Father? Of course, Sangster cannot be certain, just as I cannot be certain that Judas *did* receive forgiveness. The point, however, is clear: to claim that Judas' sin was lack of faith in the power of God's forgiveness is not sustainable. No one was there when Judas took his life – if this event even occurred, which I do not think it did – except Judas and God.

Most troubling to me is the implicit suggestion in Sangster's sermon that those who voluntarily take their own lives cannot receive forgiveness. This inference is the result of a slippery-slope argument. The assumption is that forgiveness from Jesus would have stopped Judas from killing himself. However, Judas' sorrow (some would say cowardice) was so great that he was driven to extricate himself from life rather than turn to God. Had Judas sought forgiveness from God, the argument goes, he would not have killed himself. When such an attitude is applied to all people who kill themselves voluntarily – as the case often is – there is a dangerous result. It is assumed that those who kill themselves could have prevented the act had their faith been stronger. Furthermore, it is assumed that God *cannot*, by definition, have extended forgiveness to a suicide because, had forgiveness been granted, the person would not be dead. Such beliefs are theologically disturbing and existentially dangerous.

I am not an advocate of voluntary death. Rather, I am a defender of a person's right to end his or her own life. I am also a Jesus-believer who finds nothing in my sacred scriptures to indicate that God abhors those who kill themselves. Instead, those who claim to do the work of God and champion the causes of love, forgiveness and peace, often expend great amounts of energy denouncing those who have ended their own lives. In many ways, these individuals who condemn are limiting the power of God's grace and forgiveness, because they think it impossible that God could allow a forgiven person to end his or her own life. Now, I do not encourage anyone to choose voluntary death. By the same token, I do not put it outside God's authority or prerogative to lead a person to death by their own hand. Personally, I do not have the arrogance to claim I know what God can and cannot do.

As I stated earlier in this book, it was never my intention to produce an exhaustive investigation of the various causes, issues and nuances of what might lead a person to end his or her own life. There are a great number of books written by individuals more educated and better informed about human psychology than I, and I would never pretend to offer a detailed understanding of these issues. However, I do find it troubling that almost every book written about voluntary death makes the absolutist claim that an individual must be mentally disturbed to commit such an act. As we have seen, this was not the case in ancient society. In many non-Western cultures, voluntary death is a reasonable, honorable manner in which to leave this realm. I do not feel compelled to refer people to books and sources that continue to perpetuate Western stereotypes about voluntary death.

Certainly, my own brother was mentally disturbed. When I read the journals he wrote at the peak of his illness, my heart aches with sorrow for him. Trapped within the prison of his own mind, Stephen lost a large majority of his capacity for reason. But he received the "treatment" available to him; medical science presented all it had to offer. He was diagnosed by the same doctors and therapists who write so much about voluntary death and mental illness, the same doctors who were forced to tell my family that almost every paranoid schizophrenic patient dies at his or her own hand because something drives the schizophrenic to commit the act. Stephen pursued the doctors' course of medication and therapy, and under their care he made the decision to end his life. I cannot say it was a reasoned decision; however, I cannot say it was unreasonable either.

When the so-called experts admit they know nothing, ancient theories that God can provide an individual with the *anangke* calling them home do not seem so far-fetched. In fact, they seem more reasonable than locking a person in a hospital for fifty years in order to protect the "sanctity" of life. For this reason, I do not conduct a literature review of books written by "experts" in the field of psychiatry. Rather, I show that the issue is much more complicated and involves a variety of issues they often do not consider. Perhaps we can begin to understand that science, like religion, does not always provide the answer. With that realization, maybe books such as this one will not have to be written.

Epilogue

Deciding what to do with Stephen's mortal remains was not easy. He did not leave a Last Will and Testament, so it was up to the family to make the final arrangements. Those days in mid-October are almost a blur now; I am not certain how I managed to put one foot in front of the other, much less how I made the arrangements for Stephen's wake, burial method and the memorial fund of which I am now the trustee. I certainly had help from my wife and other members of the family, but much of the task fell to me, and it was one I accepted gratefully. For the first time in my life, I was able to take care of my older brother.

We decided to have Stephen cremated, for two reasons. One, my family feels strongly that burial is a barbaric ritual; the thought of filling his body with embalming fluid and placing it to rest in an airtight container as though waiting to wake up, horrified us. (Even now, as a Christian, I do not believe in the final bodily resurrection of believers.) Two, we were ambivalent about approaching cemeteries, considering the cause of Stephen's death. Although attitudes have improved, as public awareness of the complicated nature of voluntary death has increased, many graveyards still have policies against interring the bodies of those who have taken their own lives. Cremation allowed us to deal with Stephen's remains privately and without having to deal with ignorance and ridicule.

Or so we thought.

I remember calling the only funeral home in town because it was a familiar fixture on the town's main drag. Up until about three years before Stephen's passing, the home had been a family-owned operation. Then it was purchased by a provider who had several different locations in the tri-county area. Subconsciously, I hoped that the small-town attitude had transferred from one owner to the other. It certainly had not.

On the phone we were received cordially; a time was arranged when I could meet with the director of the funeral home. I remember it was a Friday, less than thirty-six hours after we had learned about Stephen's death. That Friday was a busy day. I had been up since dawn. By the time I arrived at the funeral home meeting, I had just finished making the arrangements for Stephen's memorial service, which was to be held at the campus of my alma mater. I remember walking out of the cool, crisp October air into the sterile confines of the funeral home, the smell of artificial air-freshener not doing much to cover up the odor of the mortician's chemicals. I had walked by the building thousands of times in my seventeen years as a resident of the town and had always wondered what the inside of the building looked like. Inside the foyer I distinctly remember wishing I had been endowed with enough sense to know that some things are best left unknown.

My wife and I were greeted by the director of the funeral home and I began filling out the necessary paperwork. I had Stephen's social security number written down on a piece of paper clutched damply in my hand; my throat was dry and my eyes tired. The voice of the director seemed far away, as though these events were taking place in a movie that I was watching with only partial, drowsy interest. At the time I had cried only twice, right after the phone call from the police chief and then when I first saw my mother. In the funeral home I did not feel the desire to weep, only to expedite the procedure. Stephen's death had become a chore to which I must attend.

The funeral director asked the usual questions about Stephen's life. He made small talk, establishing that he was a member of the same philanthropic organization as my uncle; he told an asinine story about fire grilling chickens during a rainstorm at a long-ago county fair. My memories of the exact events are hazy. What I do recall is that when he looked at the coroner's report his eyes widened. He remarked, "I see the death was . . . sudden." I nodded my head, waiting for him to offer his condolences. None were extended. I completed the necessary steps and was assured that the funeral home would contact my parents or me within a few days so we could collect Stephen's mortal remains.

Well over a week later, we still had not heard from the funeral home. The wake had already been held, the flowers given by family and friends were wilting in their pots and the bereavement casseroles had either been eaten or placed in the freezer. I went back to school because it was all that I knew; when academics suffer a blow, they read and study. Our family members, in our own ways, did what we could to get through each day. We were in a holding pattern, waiting for Stephen's remains to be given to us so we could place him in his room, where his shoes were still lined up and his mail sat unopened on his desk, just as he had left them. Several calls to the funeral home went unanswered, and when my mother finally connected to a receptionist she was treated rudely. They wanted us to drive up to their home office, nearly twenty miles away, because that was where the remains were and there was not a permanent staff person at the home in Yellow Springs. My mother refused, telling them that if they did not want the business of those in our town they should not have an office located there. Finally, the funeral home agreed to meet us; they were to bring Stephen's ashes and the belongings that had been found on his body: his keys, wallet, and watch.

I am perpetually early for all appointments. I think it is a product of my neurotic nature; I feel that I am tardy if I do not arrive at least fifteen minutes early. That day was no different; we were to meet at 11:00, so I picked my mother up at 10:30 and arrived at the funeral home with twenty minutes to spare. My mom and I sat in the car and, as we had been doing quite often over the past couple weeks, talked about Stephen, how much we missed him, and wondering if we could have done anything to prevent his death. Neither of us, coincidentally, had worn a watch. I had surrendered my timepiece six years previously and vowed to never wear one again. After an excruciatingly long wait, we estimated that the time of the meeting had come and gone. I started the car and drove to a nearby payphone; Mom called the funeral home from the front steps of the public library. I could tell by her body language that the news was disturbing. While a normally peaceful and soft-spoken person, when crossed my mother can become acerbic; as she walked back to the car, I could see from her furrowed brow and pursed lips that she was upset.

"What happened?" I asked.

"They forgot."

"What?!"

"They *forgot*," the sarcasm in her voice palpable. "They'll meet us at 1:00."

"Did they at least apologize?"

"No."

I cannot recall being more upset in my life. Ironically, I had thought the most upset I could ever be had come on the day of Stephen's wake, when we had arrived at the venue and found that no chairs or tables had been set up, per our agreement. I approached the first person I saw and demanded to know why the room was not ready for us; I was lectured by this person as to how they were shorthanded because two people had not shown up to work. Standing in front of the man who was sighing heavily and acting as though I should feel pity for his inconvenience, I was overcome by anger and frustration about how selfish people can be. I explained to him that I had over sixty people coming to a memorial service for my dead brother in less than an hour and that I could not care less about his labor problems. If not for the calming influence of my wife, I would have erupted then and there. At the time I was able to chalk the experience up to individual ignorance; the man did not matter to me, and in the long run Stephen's memorial service was the tasteful and cathartic event we had hoped it would be.

When it came to the funeral home, however, I could not be as diplomatic. The only job they had was to deliver the ashes to us, an honor for which my family was paying $1,600.00; their only job was to make sure that the process was as dignified and expeditious as possible, a responsibility at which they were failing miserably. My mother and I stewed for two hours, drinking wine and venting our anger. I vowed to her that I was going to give the funeral director a tongue lashing, friend of my uncle or not. At 12:30 we packed into the car and drove back to the funeral home. This time we waited for only ten minutes. A mid-sized sedan drove into the parking lot and a man I had never seen got out. He walked up to the front door of the funeral home and attempted to open the front door, which of course was locked. I watched in horror thinking to myself that he was certainly going to reach into his pocket and pull out some keys. Indeed, the man reached into his pocket, but he did not pull out keys; instead, he removed a cell phone and placed a call. The conversation was perfunctory. My mother and I sat in stunned, expectant silence, both morbidly certain that our dignity and the dignity of Stephen were about to be trodden upon. I muttered an expletive and removed the keys from the ignition. Not thinking, I said, "The ashes are in there and he doesn't have the keys."

We got out of the car and the man sheepishly approached us. He stammered that the door was supposed to be unlocked and that he did not have the keys. Then, without pausing, he reached into his car and awkwardly handed me a box.

"Here are the ashes."

I stood there in a parking lot, cars driving by and a light snow starting to fall, holding the remains of my brother. The man produced a manila envelope, which he said contained the items found on Stephen's body, and gave them to my mother. Then he handed her a credit card slip and asked her to sign. I know for certain that he offered her no clipboard; I cannot remember if my mother was forced to sign on the box holding Stephen's ashes or the envelope she was holding. (My mother remembers signing on Stephen's ashes.) I was flabbergasted and for the first time in my life, I literally saw red. I shall never forget that my mother looked at me with deeply wounded, confused eyes. She had just lost her eldest son, the boy she had not only given birth to, but had taken into her home when a vicious illness ravaged his life and left him a shadow of his former self. There, in that parking lot, my mother suffered a great indignity, and I was powerless to stop it.

I stammered a few meaningless statements about how we were outraged; I cannot remember the specifics of what I said. I know that the diatribe I unleashed an hour later in my parents' home, no person from the funeral home anywhere around, was much more heated and better worded than what I actually said in the parking lot, but I do remember telling him that we felt as though the funeral home did not care about Stephen's death, that they regarded it as routine, but that it most certainly was not routine to us. He tried to assure me that such was not the case, but his protests did nothing to salve the wounds.

To this day, my mother and I both feel that Stephen's remains were handled in such an inconsiderate way because there is an attitude, held even by those in the business of death, that people who commit suicide do not deserve the same respect as others. I talked quite a bit about threatening to sue the funeral home, of writing them a letter telling them off, but in the end I did neither. To this day a customer service survey they had the audacity to send three weeks later sits in a box containing the paperwork associated with Stephen's death. As the three-year anniversary of Stephen's death approaches, I am thinking about writing that letter.

Appendices

Excursus One

Judas Iscariot: what's in a name?

> Then he [Jesus] goes up on the mountain and summons those he wanted, and they came to him. He formed a group of twelve to be his companions, and to be sent out to speak, and to have authority to drive out demons. And to Simon he gave the nickname Rock, and to James, the son of Zebedee, and to John, his brother, he also gave the nickname Boanerges, which means "Thunder Brothers"; and Andrew and Philip and Bartholomew and Matthew and Thomas and James, the son of Alphaeus; and Thaddeus and Simon the Zealot; and Judas Iscariot, who, in the end, turned him in.[1]

In Mark's third chapter we are introduced to the disciples collectively for the first time. Notice how they are introduced: James and John are named in relation to their father,[2] and are also given a joint nickname (and what a colorful nickname it is that is bestowed upon them!); Simon, too, has a nickname, Rock; the second James is also named in terms of his father; the second Simon is identified as the Zealot;[3] and Judas has an unexplained second name but is also introduced as the one who hands Jesus over.[4] The other names are either explained or self-explanatory, but not Iscariot. Why not? Having been told the truth about Jesus in Mk 1:1 – that he is "the Anointed" of God – it is difficult not to have an emotional reaction to being informed that Jesus is turned in by one of his boon companions. The reader is automatically prejudiced against Judas after reading his introduction. In fact, the name Judas in itself is likely to incite prejudice.

JUDAS

Though the name Judas is largely reviled in today's culture, due solely to the figure of Judas Iscariot, such was not the case in the ancient world. Klassen observes that "In the first century of the common era, two names were frequently given to young boys in Jewish families. In English, those names are Jesus and Judas."[5] The name Judas is of central importance to the history and identity of the Jewish people (it is the name of one of the twelve patriarchs and the name upon which "Jew" is founded), and remains a common name today in the form of Yehudah (Judah). There are eight different figures named Judas mentioned in the NT,[6] with heroes such as Judas Maccabeus playing important roles in the Hebrew scriptures.

Unfortunately, the name Judas has been rendered wholly unusable in the English tradition, and a more insidious detail has also emerged: the name Judas has become synonymous with "Jew," and the Judas tradition that emerges from the gospel texts has been used to justify anti-Semitism for centuries. Hyam Maccoby states:

> Nowhere in the Gospels is Judas said to be a representative of the Jewish people as a whole; yet there is an extraordinary thematic echo between the story of individual betrayal by a close disciple, and the story of communal betrayal by Jesus' blood-relatives the Jews. This resonance affects every reader of the Gospels, whether he is conscious of it or not.[7]

It is important to note that this detail is *not* a result of the gospel narratives themselves, but of later Christian tradition. Augustine argued that in the gospels Peter represents the Church and Judas the Jews.[8] Such a view quickly entered into the common Christian understanding and was still evident well into the twentieth century. As the famous German Protestant martyr Dietrich Bonhoeffer once remarked in a sermon:

> Who is Judas? Shouldn't we ask here also about the name which he carries? "Judas," doesn't it stand here for that deeply divided people of Jesus' origin, for the elect people, which had received the promise of the Messiah and yet rejected it? For the people of Judas, which loved the Messiah and yet could not love him thus. "Judas"— in German the name means "Thank." Was his kiss not the thanks brought to Jesus by the divided people of the disciple and yet at the same time its eternal renunciation?[9]

Bonhoeffer's remarks operate on the assumption that it was the intention of the *gospel writers* to depict Judas as the only "Jew" within Jesus' circle of followers. If this argument is to hold, we must understand the premises upon which it is built.

Judaism was by no means uniform during the time of Jesus; indeed, there were many ways of being "Jewish." However, a look at European Christian art from the medieval times to the twenty-first century demonstrates that Jesus and his apostles (except for Judas, who is almost always painted with exaggerated Semitic features) were all depicted as white men with purely Occidental features. In this way, Jesus and his apostles are denied their *Jewish* heritage and are captured in popular iconography as embodying European ideals. Such a development takes many centuries, however, and could not have been the intention of the gospel writers. Those who view Judas as the only "Jew" in the Jesus movement do so with anachronistic criteria completely alien to the milieu of the ancient world.

Another possibility for understanding Judas' first name, and one which warrants our attention, is that Judas was the only Judean in the group of apostles.[10] Most theories supporting this claim are based upon analyses of Judas' surname as well, which I discuss at length below. However, there are two more immediate observations that can be made. One, Mark's gospel was written to proclaim Jesus as the *Jewish* Messiah (8:27), who, according to First Isaiah, would come from the line of David (Isa 9:6–7). Whether or not this proclamation of being the Messiah came from the historical Jesus or not is unimportant; what is important is that the Markan community does not appear to have antipathy toward the idea of Jesus being the fulfillment of a Judean prophecy. If it was the intention of the Markan author/community to castigate Judeans, why would the community understand Jesus in these terms? Two, understanding Judas as the only disciple from Judea presupposes a division between the "Jews" and "Christians." Not only had "Christianity" not yet developed, but also there is *no* historical evidence to show us that a definitive split had occurred between the Jesus-followers and the Jewish faith by 70 CE. To suggest that Mark was attempting to castigate Jews as a whole is not historically sound because it presupposes "Christianity" as a distinct religion already in existence.

However, we must remain open to the possibility that Judas, whether historically or metaphorically, embodies "Jewish" characteristics rejected by the Jesus movement. Mark's use of names is highly significant: Simon Peter as the "rock" seems sarcastic; Barabbas properly translates to "Son of the Father." The crowd chooses the wrong son, further highlighting the guilt of those who reject Jesus. It is possible that "Judas" is meant to represent those "Jews" who reject Jesus, but I do not find enough evidence from the first century to maintain that Mark meant to castigate the Jews as a whole.

ISCARIOT

The name Iscariot is even more complicated and controversial than the name Judas. It appears ten times in the NT with five different variations.[11] For our purposes it will suffice to name the four most prevalent interpretations and discuss the relevant issues.

1. The first interpretation holds that "Iscariot" refers to the town in which Judas was from, possibly Kerioth (Joshua 15:25), and uses this as evidence that Judas was the only Judean (person from Judah, or the southern Jewish kingdom). Others agree that the Hebrew *ish* found in "Iscariot" indicates that the surname designates a place, but argue for either Askaroth or Askar, near Schechem. Etymological objections render this option "dubious."[12] On the other hand, some have argued that one should not look to the Hebrew *ish* but to the Aramaic word *keriotha*, which would indicate that Judas is from Jerusalem.[13] The problem with this theory is that it is based on a selective transliteration of the NT Greek into the original Aramaic, making it unlikely that the interpretation is sound. Of the two questionable options, I find the first most troublesome. To argue that the name "Judas" automatically means that one is from Judea and that "Iscariot" indicates being from Kerioth, or any other southern town, is not verifiable historically and is oftentimes used by those who champion anti-Semitic agendas.

2. The second interpretation holds that the Hebrew term *shachar*, meaning "false one," is at the root of "Iscariot."[14] If so, the term would be pejorative and would refer to Judas' perceived character and not his historical name. We must be wary of believing this theory because it is directly dependent on viewing Judas as a treacherous person, a detail that cannot be found in the gospel traditions, but in later Christian hermeneutics.

3. The third interpretation for Judas' name depends on his perceived actions. The Hebrew root *sakar* ("deliverer") is thought to fit into *(I)skariot(h)*. The argument holds that just as the Greek *paradidōmi* describes Judas' act, so is his Hebrew name a literal translation of *(I)skariot*, "the one handing over."[15] Once again, if this be true, then it is not Judas' historical name but a designation given him after his death.

4. The final interpretation we shall discuss holds that Judas belonged to a group called the Sicarii (so called for the short daggers, or

sicae, they carried), Jewish assassins active during the time of Josephus and known for their habit of executing high-ranking officials in very public, yet crowded, places. It is thought by those who take this position that the Sicarii were a branch of the Zealots. There are problems with this theory. First, etymological discrepancies regarding how the Greek *sikarion* becomes "Iscariot" make it unlikely.[16] Second, the evidence we have from Josephus[17] contradicts itself, making it impossible to know for sure when the Sicarii, like the Zealots, were active.[18] Third, why would Judas not be arrested by the Temple officials with whom he supposedly colludes? If Judas was part of a dangerous group involved with political subversion, certainly the Temple officials would have an interest in detaining him. Those who might argue that Judas' activities came after the death of Jesus resort to special pleading, for only Matthew and Luke–Acts speak of Judas after the "handing over" and both of these narratives kill Judas off. There is simply no evidence to support this theory.

As frustrating and unsatisfying as it is, we simply do not know what Judas' name or surname means or meant to the original audience; as Klassen states, "there is no certain answer."[19] It is possible that the title "Iscariot" was attributed to Judas posthumously. Klassen remarks that "If those who suggest that the term Iscariot came into use only after Judas' death are right, then it is also possible that not even the early evangelists knew what Iscariot meant."[20]

Excursus Two
Judas as an historical figure

> The criterion of embarrassment clearly comes into play . . . for there is
> no cogent reason why the early church should have gone out of its way
> to invent such a troubling tradition as Jesus' betrayal by Judas, one of
> his chosen Twelve. Why the church should have expended so much
> effort to create a story that it immediately had to struggle to explain
> away defies all logic. Rather, Jesus' betrayal by Judas, a member of the
> intimate circle of the Twelve, called for an explanation and so called
> forth OT texts to soften the shock.
>
> John Meier[1]

In regard to the historicity of Judas, biblical scholar John Meier and
I stand on opposite ends of the spectrum: he argues that Judas was an
historical figure because of the "criterion of embarrassment," whereas
I argue that Judas was a creation of the Markan community meant to
undercut the authority of the twelve. The reader is already familiar
with my theory; it is important to give adequate treatment to Meier's.
Loosely stated, the criterion of embarrassment holds that because the
story of Judas reflects poorly upon the twelve (and perhaps upon Jesus
as well), it must be true. He argues that the historical Judas turned Jesus
in and that early Jesus-followers, struggling to make sense of this act,
called upon passages and prophecies from the Hebrew scriptures.
Meier writes that "Jesus being handed over by Judas thus parallels Jesus'
death in a basic way: the shocking fact calls forth the Scripture texts –
not vice versa. The betrayal by Judas is no more a creation of OT
[Hebrew Bible] prophecy used apologetically than is Jesus' death."[2] This
is a substantive objection, but one I reject out of hand.

First, Meier argues that Judas as a member of the twelve is
"historical fact due to multiple attestation."[3] However, this multiple
attestation is achieved only by use of Mark; while Meier argues that the

Notes

1 The legacy of Augustine

1 Augustine of Hippo, *Concerning the City of God, Against the Pagans*, trans. by Henry Bettenson, New York: Penguin Books, 1984, Book 1, Chapter 17.
2 Augustine of Hippo, *Confessions*, trans. by R.S. Pinecoffin, New York: Penguin Books, 1961, 7.12.
3 William C. Placher, *A History of Christian Theology: An Introduction*, Philadelphia: The Westminster Press, 1983, p. 108.

2 The earliest levels of the written Christian tradition: Paul and Q

1 William Klassen, *Judas: Betrayer or Friend of Jesus?* London: Augsburg Fortress, 1996, p. 51.
2 Unfortunately, the true meaning of "Christ" is unknown to a large majority of Christians. The term *Christos*, meaning "Anointed," is the Greek rendering of the Hebrew word *Mashiah*. Many think "Christ" is Jesus' surname, when in fact nothing could be further from the truth. The term is derived from the ancient Israelite practice of putting oil on, or anointing, the heads of kings at coronation ceremonies. Therefore a christ is one who has been anointed by God as king: King Saul and King David were both "christs." In the Roman tradition, Caesar was a christ. As such, in this treatment Jesus shall be referred to as Jesus the Anointed.
3 The Pharisees were a group of scholars whose expertise was in the area of Jewish Canon Law.
4 Arthur J. Dewey notes in an unpublished work: "[W]hile most Christians have heard much of Paul, few have had the opportunity to understand him in his world. Usually we hear snippets from a letter of Paul—like some briefly overheard conversation—but are at a loss as to know where he's going. We have no idea of Paul's overall perspective, little notion of the concerns out of which he wrote. . . . Instead of closely reading [Paul] . . . we usually settle for prepackaged platitudes." Used by permission of the author.
5 *Paredōka* is the first person Aorist Active form (that is the first person having performed an action in the past); hence "I gave over"; *paredidōto* is third person, Imperfect Middle Passive (that is, the action was performed on the agent in the past), hence, "was handed over." It should be noted that

the word *paradidōmi* is in the first person and is therefore properly translated "I hand over," however it shall be referred to forthwith without reference to person, that is "hand over."

6 William Klassen's work *Judas: Betrayer or Friend of Jesus?* is a valuable resource for those who wish to be introduced to the relevant issues pertinent to historical Judas scholarship. While I disagree with some of Klassen's conclusions, as I will demonstrate in my own conclusions, I am indebted to his meticulous research and detailed presentation, specifically in relation to the discussion of *paradidōmi*, pp. 47–58.

7 Ibid., p. 48.

8 Ibid., p. 47.

9 Septuagint means "the seventy." For this reason the Roman numerals are used as a symbol for the text. Legend holds that seventy (or seventy-two) leading scholars were commissioned by Ptolemy Philadelphus around 125 BCE to provide a Greek translation of the Hebrew Bible. Legend also holds that the scholars, all in separate rooms, emerged after seventy-two days with exactly the same translation. Anyone who has done translations of their own knows such an event is highly unlikely.

10 Josephus claims he begged the beleaguered Jews not to kill themselves, arguing that suicide is wrong. However, he does not claim it is a "sin."

11 Flavius Josephus, *The Jewish War*, trans. by H.St.J. Thackery, Cambridge: Loeb Classical Libraries, 1967, 3.316–92.

12 Klassen, op. cit., p. 49.

13 Quoted from Klassen, op. cit., p. 47.

14 Ibid., p. 47.

15 Ibid., p. 51.

16 Ibid., p. 50.

17 While Vatican II certainly opened the door even wider to Catholic biblical scholars, the most important advance was made some twenty years earlier when Pius XII issued the encyclical *Divino Afflante Spiritu*, which advocated a responsible, informed examination of Scripture (albeit under the guise of papal control).

18 Matthew, Mark and Luke are commonly called the Synoptics, literally meaning "with one eye." They are so called because, in contrast to the Johannine narrative, they have so many similarities in language and structure that they seem to have a close literary relationship.

19 For an excellent discussion of Weisse's career and his impact upon biblical scholarship, see Albert Schweitzer's definitive work, *The Quest of the Historical Jesus: A Critical Study of Its Progress From Reimarus to Wrede*, 4th edn, New York: Macmillan, 1948, pp. 121–36.

20 While the names attached to the gospels indicate a certitude about authorship, we actually do not know who wrote the documents. The names were assigned to the gospels years after they were written. For the sake of clarity I will refer to them by the common designates, but the reader must keep this caveat in mind: I refer to the text, not to the specific individual who is credited with writing the gospel.

21 Augustine writes, "Mark followed him [Matthew] like a slave and seems his summarizer." See *On the Agreement of the Evangelists*, 1.2.4, in Sean P. Kealy's translation in *Mark's Gospel: A History of Its Interpretation*, Ramsey, NJ: Paulist Press, 1982, p. 82.

22 It is also interesting to note that Matthew retains Mark's intercalated (inserted) story, the aforementioned tale of the hemorrhaging woman.

23 See, for example, Jesus being tempted by the devil: Mark 1:12–13//Matt. 4:1–11//Luke 4:1–13.

24 A few scholars reject the existence of Q. John Shelby Spong challenges mainstream Q scholarship in an interesting manner. He writes "Q is, in my opinion, a Matthean creation" (*Liberating the Gospels: Reading the Bible with Jewish Eyes*, San Francisco: HarperCollins, 1996, p. 107). Even though he states in a footnote that disproving Q is beyond the scope of his present treatment, he argues that Matthew leans "heavily on Paul" and cites numerous texts to support this theory. While I find Spong's work to be an important weapon against fundamentalism and literalism, his connections between the epistles of Paul and Matthew's Gospel are tenuous at best. Dispensing with common theories regarding Q not only undercuts the efficacy of most historical Jesus scholarship but biblical scholarship as a whole, and therefore should not be undertaken lightly; in order to replace one valid theory, another of better credence must be offered, a criterion Spong does not fulfill. I see no relationship between Q and the epistles of Paul.

25 All the original NT writings were composed in Greek, and scholars argue that Q was written in Greek as well. One should keep in mind that Jesus and his followers most likely spoke Aramaic, though some argue that they must have known some Greek to function in the larger Hellenistic world. Arguments that Jesus spoke Latin do not, in my opinion, have any basis in fact: the Eastern Roman Empire remained largely Greek and Semitic-speaking for decades after the death of Jesus.

26 It should be noted that traders and those in business often did know how to write, at least basic contracts and legal agreements. Archeology gives us a fascinating glimpse into the life of the common person through the papyri that are discovered. However, to own proper volumes written by learned sages and philosophers, or to have work of one's own circulated and read required a great deal of education and resources, which were typically reserved for the aristocratic classes.

27 John Dominic Crossan offers an outstanding treatment of oral tradition in ancient and living cultures, in his work *The Birth of Christianity: Discovering What Happened in the Years Immediately After the Execution of Jesus*, San Francisco: HarperCollins, 1998, pp. 49–84. Drawing on already conducted studies and his seemingly unlimited knowledge of the ancient world, Crossan adeptly shows that no written tradition could possibly contain the exact words of Jesus, especially since the earliest possible text dates from twenty years after his death.

28 For a detailed reconstruction and analysis of Q, see Kloppenborg *et al.*, *The Critical Edition of Q*, Minneapolis: Lewen/Fortress Press, 2000. For a more accessible and straightforward treatment, see *The Complete Gospels*, ed. Robert J. Miller, 3rd edn, Santa Rosa, Sonoma, CA: Polebridge Press, 1994, pp. 249–300; for a thorough discussion of the Q community and how contemporary Christianity is woefully ignorant of its importance, see Burton L. Mack, *The Lost Gospel: The Book of Q and Christian Origins*, San Francisco: HarperCollins, 1993.

29 The designate Coptic refers to both a language and a Christian Church in

Egypt. In the above context, however, the reference is to the language, which derives from ancient Egyptian and has many Greek accretions.

30 Miller, op. cit., pp. 301–2.

31 Mack, op. cit., pp. 195–6.

32 The parallels between Q and Thomas are many, however, and their possible relationship to one another quite complicated and involved. For an outstanding treatment of the salient issues and a learned assessment of what can be gathered from a comparison of the two, see John Dominic Crossan, *The Birth of Christianity*, pp. 239–92; see also Mack, op. cit., pp. 180–3, where he argues that the Thomas community originally belonged to the Q community, although the two split when the Q community began to understand Jesus in apocalyptic terms.

33 Wisdom motifs are sayings that concern divine Wisdom (*Sophia*). In this layer of Q, Jesus informs his followers how to live a proper life and how to know God.

34 Mack, op. cit., pp. 139–40.

35 Although I do not subscribe to all of Mack's theories, I find his analysis of the Q community convincing. In the brief discussion of the Q theology and Christology that follows, I do not discuss Mack's theories on how and why the Q community's understanding of itself and Jesus changes. However, I ask the reader to keep in mind that Jesus as a Wisdom Prophet is an interpretation that most likely evolves over a period of decades, and does not spring forth intact by the year 70 CE.

36 Luke is more faithful in its use of Q's order than Matthew, so citations of Q use the numbering of the parallel passage in Luke.

37 "And she said to the king, 'The report was true which I heard in my own land of your wisdom, but I did not believe the reports until I came and my own eyes had seen it; and behold, the half was not told me; your wisdom and prosperity surpass the report which I heard'" (1 Kings 10:6–7; RSV).

38 Miller, op. cit., p. 251.

39 Richard A. Edwards, *A Theology of Q*, Philadelphia: Fortress Press, 1976, p. 47.

40 The deuteronomic historian is responsible for the redaction, or editing, of the material in the Hebrew Bible found in Joshua–II Kings. In this corpus, Israel's constant occupations and troubles are attributed to a cycle in which things go well for a time, then Israel sins against God (usually by worshiping the Canaanite deities Baal and Ashterah), God punishes them, the people cry out, God sends a judge/prophet/Davidic king, the people repent, and the cycle repeats.

41 Arthur J. Dewey, "Can we let Jesus die?" from *The Once and Future Faith*, Santa Rosa, Sonoma, CA: Polebridge Press, 2001, p. 141.

42 Miller, op. cit., p. 251.

43 Mack, op. cit., pp. 4–5.

44 The role of the disciples in Q is discussed in greater detail below in Chapter 3, Mark: the beginning of the Judas myth.

3 Mark: the beginning of the Judas myth

1 E.P. Sanders, *The Historical Figure of Jesus*, New York: Penguin Press, 1993, p. 74.

2 As discussed in Chapter 2, the earliest form of Christian "gospel" was oral statements about Jesus, known as *kerygma*. When the gospels were written down, very few people had access to the documents themselves, but the gospels were circulated by oral transmission. It is important to remember that many early Christians encountered Jesus through the spoken word; consequently, I refer to the audience of the gospels as "listener/reader." I am not the first scholar to do so; see Janice Capel Anderson and Stephen D. Moore, *Mark and Method: New Approaches in Biblical Studies*, Minneapolis: Augsburg Fortress, 1996.

3 Anderson and Moore, op. cit., p. 7.

4 Martin Dibelius, *From Tradition to Gospel*, trans. Bertram Lee Woolf, New York: Charles Scribner's Sons, 1935, p. 3. Cited here from Anderson and Moore, op. cit., p. 7.

5 How the twelve emerge is peculiar. In Mk 3:13–19, Simon, Andrew, James and John appear once again, yet the four are not named merely as individuals, but as part of a group of "twelve" who are given the authority to speak on behalf of Jesus and to drive out demons. Seven of the eight additional members of the twelve who are introduced to the listener/reader are never mentioned as individuals again; only Judas Iscariot, named in Mk 3:19, returns as an actor (14:10–11). A discussion of Judas shall be postponed until the end of this chapter. For now, it shall suffice to point out that both the existence of the twelve and the authority of followers to cast out demons are unique to Mark; Q makes no such report.

6 See Robert Miller, "Is the Apocalyptic Jesus history?" from *The Once and Future Faith*, Santa Rosa, Sonoma, CA: Polebridge Press, 2001, pp. 101–16.

7 See Excursus One: Judas Iscariot: what's in a name? at the end of this book.

8 The theory of dyads usually refers to the significant relationship between two people, such as husband and wife. However, it can also refer to a group dynamic, because each individual person in the group chooses to associate with the other individuals. In this way, the sullied or blemished nature of one person can affect scores of others in his or her social group. I argue that the oath taken by the individual members of the twelve united them not only as a group, but also as dyads.

9 The significance of the kiss is discussed below in Chapter 5, under the heading The kiss of peace.

10 John Dominic Crossan has argued this as well. Of his two works discussing the questions, *Who Killed Jesus: Exposing the Roots of Anti-Semitism in the Gospel Story of the Death of Jesus*, San Francisco: HarperCollins, 1996, is the more accessible and cogent.

11 Arthur J. Dewey, "Can we let Jesus die?" from *The Once and Future Faith*, p. 147.

12 Ibid., p. 148.

13 Ibid., p. 150.

14 See Hyam Maccoby, *Judas Iscariot and the Myth of Jewish Evil*, New York: Free Press, 1992, pp. 43–4. While Maccoby makes a good point about the role of myth in the creation of Judas Iscariot, he goes much too far in his conclusion that Judas Iscariot, in fact, is the brother of Jesus and properly should be called "Prince Jude."

15 See Excursus One: Judas Iscariot: what's in a name? It is possible that by

giving Judas the name for Judah, the Markan community further assigns blame for the death of Jesus.

4 Whether 'tis nobler

1 Albert Camus, *The Myth of Sisyphus: And Other Essays*, trans. Justin O'Brien, New York: Vintage Books, 1955, p. 3.

2 Cesare Pavese, *The Burning Brand: Diaries, 1935–1950*, New York: Walker, 1961, p. 27.

3 Yukio Mishima, *Patriotism*, trans. Geoffery W. Sergant, New York: New Directors, 1995, p. 7.

4 This theory was voiced initially by David Daube, "The linguistics of suicide," *Philosophy and Public Affairs* (1972), 422. Information obtained from Arthur J. Droge and James D. Tabor, *A Noble Death*, San Francisco: HarperCollins, 1992, pp. 7–15.

5 Droge and Tabor, op. cit., p. 7.

6 Ibid., p. 7.

7 Ibid., p. 7.

8 Seneca, *On Anger*, 3.15.3–4; taken from Droge and Tabor, op. cit., p. 34.

9 Droge and Tabor's work, *A Noble Death*, is the definitive text about suicide in the ancient world. As they exhaustively discuss the pertinent issues, I shall highlight only the relevant details.

10 A. Alvarez, *The Savage God: A Study of Suicide*, New York: Random House, 1970, p. 77.

11 Droge and Tabor, op. cit., p. 22.

12 Ibid., p. 30.

13 Ibid., p. 36.

14 Ibid., p. 32.

15 Ibid., p. 42.

16 The death of Saul is also related in 2 Sam 1:1–16 and 1 Chronicles 10:1–7. In the former, Saul is killed out of mercy by the armor bearer, who is killed by David for slaying God's Anointed; in the latter, Saul is depicted as such an unworthy character that God himself slays Saul.

17 The original ban on suicide was made by the Catholic Church, but even after the Protestant Reformation nations such as England, France and Germany did not change their laws regarding suicide; in fact, many made them more harsh, as I discuss below.

18 A. Alvarez, op. cit., p. 45.

19 Ibid., p. 46.

20 A brief, yet detailed discussion of crucifixion practices is necessary before a comparison between the treatment of suicides and those who were crucified can be drawn. In certain Middle Eastern societies, including greater Palestine where Jesus lived, there was a practice of "dead crucifixion" – that is, hanging an already deceased person on a "tree" as a public statement (see Joshua 10:2, 26–7). "Live crucifixion" as a form of civil execution was introduced into the region by the Romans. Contrary to what many contemporary Christians might think, death by crucifixion did not come quickly. The gospel reports of Jesus' death occurring in six hours would not only be historically idiosyncratic, but highly unlikely. (Although if Jesus were scourged to the extent Mel Gibson depicts in his gruesome and troubling

film *The Passion of the Christ*, Jesus might have died quickly. However, it seems to me that no human being could have withstood such a brutal and prolonged beating.) Death happened slowly and by asphyxiation: the weight of the body eventually became too much to sustain and the internal diaphragm muscles simply fatigued and collapsed, leaving the victim unable to breath. Breaking the legs of the executed would hasten the death process, thereby weakening the body's support structure, but even then death could take several days. The Romans were aware of the brutality of crucifixion and used it to their advantage; crucifixions were not conducted outside the public eye, but in full view for all to see. In fact, they were public spectacles, forerunners to the Roman gladiatorial games, the witch burnings in Europe and seventeenth-century New England, and the lynchings of African-Americans in post-Civil-War America.

Part of the crucifixion experience was being subjected to the elements: the victim's naked body was exposed to the blazing sun, the taunts and jeers of those observing, the birds of the air pecking at the eyes and open wounds, and the beasts of the field attacking the lower body. In contrast to popular Christian iconography, crucifixes were approximately 5 feet (1.5m) high, so the crucified was not far from the ground; wild dogs kept from coming inside the city walls were able to find plenty to eat in crucifixion yards. Rats fought for what the dogs did not eat. After the victim finally expired, the corpse was usually left on the cross for the birds and the beasts to pick clean, the remaining bones bleached by the sun. The Romans meant to send a lasting message with crucifixion that did not end with the victim's death; on the contrary, those who were forced to walk past the crosses in the course of their everyday activities were constantly reminded of Rome's power. The putrid smell of death must have been overwhelming, but the effect could not be denied; all would have been aware that subversive and unacceptable activities would result in one being affixed to a cross.

Those who were crucified were typically marched naked through the town square, forced to carry the wooden crossbeams upon which they would be affixed before being lifted up by *furcillae*, or forked poles, and placed on the semi-permanent uprights that, in Roman provinces, were a common part of the landscape. Sometimes there was a placard, or *titulus*, affixed to the cross that detailed the crime a person was being crucified for; this was not, however, always done, nor was it required. Crucifixion was so public and brutal that most people got the message even if they did not, or could not, read the charge. In fact, there were literally dozens of ways one could be crucified, various crosses one could be affixed to, different positions one could be placed in, a seemingly endless series of punishments and tortures one could be subjected to before even being placed upon the cross. Despite the methodological anomalies, the underlying principle was the same: crucifixion was a brutal practice meant to legislate through terror. The average person living under Roman occupation understood this, the general attitude being: message delivered, message received.

21 Flavius Josephus, *Jewish Antiquities*, 17.10.10; no. 295. Varus killed himself by falling on his sword rather than be taken prisoner during a revolt in 9 CE; the Emperor Augustus was so upset he did not cut his hair or beard for three months, bemoaning the loss of a dear friend who had at one time saved the empire from the revolting rabble. For a more detailed account, see

Will Durant, *Caesar and Christ*, New York: Simon and Schuster, 1944, p. 218.
22 A. Alvarez, op. cit., p. 46.
23 For a detailed discussion, see Raymond Brown, *The Death of the Messiah: From Gethsemane to the Grave: A Commentary on the Passion Narratives in the Four Gospels*, 2 vols, New York: BantamDoubleday, 1994, pp. 1207–11.
24 Alvarez, op. cit., p. 46. I find it no coincidence that, in popular folklore, Judas is the first vampire.
25 After the Reformation, nations such as England increased the stringency of their laws against suicide. I think this was in large part due to the general abhorrence these nations had for the Catholic Church. Indeed, one of the most effective methods used to root out Catholicism was to seize areas that had once been under Church control. That the land and money of certain suicides went to the king and his retinue, and not the papacy, is just one example of this practice.
26 Take, for example, the actions of King James Stuart, the Scottish successor to Queen Elizabeth. On 21 April 1603, the newly anointed English monarch, on a tour of his new kingdom, summarily executed a Lincolnshire man for thievery. The man, an English citizen, was not afforded a proper trial, scandalizing James' new subjects. James was heavily criticized for circumventing the law, and in many ways never recovered from this *faux pas*. See Adam Nicolson, *God's Secretaries: The Making of the King James Bible*, New York: HarperCollins, 2003, pp. 14–15.
27 Alvarez, op. cit., p. 46.
28 William Shakespeare, *The Tragedy of Hamlet, Prince of Denmark*, III:i.

5 The growth of a myth: Judas in Matthew

1 John Calvin, *Harmony of the Evangelists*, Grand Rapids, MI: Baker Books, 2002, XVI:255–6.
2 It would be anachronistic to think of these early adherents as "Christians." Arguably, Christianity as it is popularly understood was not born until the conversion of Constantine and the convening of the Council of Niceae in 325 CE.
3 Some would argue that this is not the case, given Mt 10:23. However, I think it is significant that Matthew retains this prophecy, suggesting that the passage may not have required a literal understanding. As such, Mt 24 and 25, which discuss the Parousia, may be intended as metaphorical declarations. See Stephen Harris, *The New Testament: A Student's Introduction*, 4th edn, New York: McGraw Hill, 2002, p. 165.
4 Again, scholars are unsure of where Matthew's gospel was written. A widely accepted estimate is Antioch, Syria. In all likelihood, the Matthean community was composed of Jewish Christians (Jesus-believers) and Gentiles who were Torah-observant. See Harris, op. cit., p. 148.
5 In the original Hebrew, the word commonly translated as "virgin" is more accurately translated as "a young woman" (*'almah*). The confusion arose when the Hebrew Bible was translated into Greek (the Septuagint or LXX) and the Greek word for virgin (*parthenos*) was substituted. The passage indicates to scholars that Matthew was familiar with the LXX, not the Hebrew text. An excellent translation is to be found in the Jewish Publication

Society's Tanakh: "Assuredly, my Lord will give you a sign of His own accord! Look, the young woman is with child and about to give birth to a son."

6   John Shelby Spong, in *Liberating the Gospels: Reading the Bible with Jewish Eyes*, San Francisco: HarperCollins, 1996, makes a compelling argument that Joseph was not a historical figure but rather a midrashic (the result of commentary) creation intended to provide Jesus with a direct link to David, thus supporting the Matthean community's christology and soteriology, and bringing to the mind of the listener/reader other central figures of Israel's history, such as Jacob (the father of the heads of the "twelve tribes") and Joseph (the most beloved of Jacob's sons). See pp. 219–232.

7   In the late eighth century BCE, the Davidic monarchy was in danger of falling as the result of an alliance between Israel and Syria; Ahaz, the new king of Judah, found himself under attack. Fearful that Jerusalem would fall, Ahaz did not know what to do. God, angered by Israel's alliance with Syria, assured Ahaz that the Davidic monarchy would be sustained and that Syria would be vanquished. God asked Ahaz if he wanted a sign; Ahaz said "No," but God gave one anyway, that "a young woman shall conceive . . ." Immanuel, meaning "God is with us" was to be born immediately as a sign of God's pledge to protect Judah and defeat Syria.

8   Harris, op. cit., p. 149.

9   One of Jesus' brothers also is named Simon (Mk 3:3); note that a certain Judas is also named as a brother.

10   Note that the "messianic secret" is repeated in v.20, further proof that Matthew used Mark as a source.

11   See Raymond Brown, *The Death of the Messiah: From Gethsemane to the Grave: A Commentary on the Passion Narratives in the Four Gospels*, 2 vols., New York: BantamDoubleday, 1994, pp. 1:639–40.

12   While I find this to be an important question, we must proceed with caution. It is far too easy to read St Anselm's theory of satisfaction into this passage, a christological and soteriological idea that took many centuries and a number of Church Councils to produce. However, the idea of freeing one from the constraints of society and the tyranny of leadership (the Pharisees) is central to Matthew's gospel. There may be a tenuous connection between the price of a slave, Jesus' salvific act and the special-M material. Ultimately, however, we cannot know with any certainty.

13   William Klassen, *Judas: Betrayer or Friend of Jesus?*, London: Augsburg Fortress, 1996, p. 226.

14   The greatest example is that of Joseph the Righteous, who plays informer on his brothers, returning to their father a bad report regarding his brothers' behavior. The brothers react strongly, eventually selling Joseph into slavery (Gen 37:1–36). A later midrashic text states that the specific amount was thirty silver pieces. Klassen, ibid., pp. 63–6.

15   Ibid., p. 64.

16   Frank Morrison, *Who Moved the Stone?*, London: Faber, 1930, p. 37.

17   Matthew adds that it is the hand (*cheira*) that dips.

18   It is immediately significant that Judas is not identified as "Judas Iscariot, one of the twelve." Once again, I take this as evidence that the Matthean community supports the authority of the twelve and, through subtle

changes, places sole responsibility for Jesus being handed over upon Judas Iscariot, attempting to distance Judas from the twelve.

19 Karl Barth, *Church Dogmatics*, Edinburgh: T. & T. Clark, 1957, p. 467; quoted from Klassen, op. cit., p. 186.

20 Cf. Jer 26:15, Ps 106:38–39, II Kings 24:4, Deut 21:9 and Deut 27:25.

21 Klassen, op. cit., p. 163.

22 Ibid., p. 164.

23 Brown, op. cit., p. 641.

24 See ibid., pp. 642–4 for a detailed discussion.

25 My italics, NRSV.

26 Flavius Josephus, *Antiquities*, translated by Louis H. Feldman, Cambridge: Loeb Classical Libraries, 1965, pp. 228–9, describes Ahithophel as regarding voluntary death as superior to facing a punishment later.

27 Brown, op. cit., p. 647.

28 Ibid., p. 646.

29 Ibid., p. 647.

30 Dr Arthur Dewey, delivering a lecture at Xavier University in July 2004, observed that the Blood Curse is dramatic irony: the blood, poured out for the "forgiveness of sins" (26:27), is the very blood the people call to be upon them and their children. In rejecting Jesus, they are inadvertently saved.

6 Luke–Acts: Judas as Satan

1 Lao Tzu, *The Way of Life*, trans. Witter Bynner, New York: Perigree Books, 1944, p. 35.

2 See John Shelby Spong, "Seeking the Jewish clue that will unlock the third gospel," from *Liberating the Gospels: Reading the Bible with Jewish Eyes*, San Francisco: HarperCollins, 1996, pp. 119–65.

3 Notice that Simon has not yet been called "Peter" by Jesus, but Luke uses the nickname anyway.

4 A considerable amount of imaginative thinking has been dedicated to the presence of two disciples named Judas. Perhaps the most ludicrous theory has been offered by Hyam Maccoby in *Judas Iscariot and the Myth of Jewish Evil*, New York: Free Press, 1992. After claiming that "Judas Iscariot was Jesus' brother" (p. 146), Maccoby states that "Luke splits Judas into two: the evil Judas and the innocuous 'brother of James'. The name Iscariot is allotted to the evil Judas. From now on, there are two Judases" (p. 150). Through the use of uncited, questionable evidence, Maccoby concludes that "Judas was actually the third 'Bishop' (or more correctly, Vice-Regent) of Jerusalem 'Church'. Such an appointment is only what one would expect, given the royalist position of the group. What better candidate for leadership, pending the return of King Jesus, than his brother, Prince Judas Iscariot?" (p. 156). Such an outlandish theory does nothing to help us understand the early Jesus communities, nor does it place us any closer to comprehending the role of Judas Iscariot in the Christian traditions.

5 See Chapter 3, under subheading Q and Mark: how is one a follower of Jesus?

6 Though the directions are given explicitly to the seventy-two, they are also implicitly given to the twelve. In Lk 22:35–8, Jesus refers to these instructions when addressing the twelve. Curiously, he reverses them as he faces

arrest, thus linking his directives with a fulfillment of the scriptures. There is a shift from the Matthean emphasis on constant non-violence: according to Luke, there is a time for the sword.

7 See, for example, Lk 17:1–6: Jesus is admonishing his disciples to be on their guard, and the apostles answer, "Make our trust grow" (v.5). Are these members of the seventy-two who are sent out, or members of the twelve, named apostles? The twelve exist as a substantive group throughout the gospel, so there is no need to belabor a point that may be insignificant. I draw the reader's attention to the changes because of the existence of the seventy-two. The community of Luke–Acts seems to have been highly organized and hierarchical; it is possible that within this community there were differences between "disciples" and "apostles." Discerning these differences, however, relies upon too much conjecture.

8 The Cohen brothers' film *O Brother, Where Art Thou?* treats this common belief in an exceedingly humorous way. Tommy Johnson (meant to be the blues legend of the same name), who sold his soul to the devil in order to play the guitar, explains to the three main characters that the devil (Satan) is in fact a white man with a deep voice who is accompanied by a hell-hound.

9 Elaine Pagels, *The Origin of Satan*, New York: Random House, 1995, p. 39.

10 Burton L. Mack, *The Lost Gospel: The Book of Q and Christian Origins*, San Francisco: HarperCollins, 1993, p. 82. The *diablos* role is similar to that played by *satan* in the Book of Job.

11 Ibid., pp. 59–62

12 Ibid., p. 59.

13 Ibid., pp. 60–1.

14 Mack argues that the testing material dates from the third, or latest, level of Q, reflecting a more developed community.

15 For Matthew, the chief enemies are the Pharisees, who as a group denounce and reject Jesus, acting as the primary stumbling block and adversary to his mission. Luke, as is discussed below, does not issue a wholesale condemnation of the Pharisees, but rather describes Herod and Judas as the primary adversaries.

16 For a detailed discussion, see Pagels, op. cit., pp. 91–3.

17 This is the second passage in which Peter is called Simon (cf. Lk 24:36). I do not know if there is significance to this detail. If he were not called Simon after seeing Jesus resurrected, I would argue that he once again becomes "Peter" after recovering from his loss of faith. However, such a position is not supported by the evidence; Simon is called Peter in v.34.

18 The reader should note that Luke adds an important addendum to Peter's oath, saying he will follow Jesus all the way to prison (*phulakēn*).

19 NRSV; *The Oxford Annotated* notes the translation discrepancy.

20 This connection was first made by William Klassen, *Judas: Betrayer or Friend of Jesus?* London: Augsburg Fortress, 1996, p. 169.

21 William C. Placher, *Readings in the History of Christian Theology, Volume One: From Its Beginnings to the Eve of the Reformation*, Philadelphia: Westminster Press, 1988, pp. 17–18.

22 Klassen, op. cit., p. 173.

7 Conclusions

1 Peter J. Boyle, "The Jesus war," *New Yorker*, 15 September 2003, pp. 66–7.
2 Warren W. Wiersbe, ed., *Classic Sermons on Judas Iscariot*, Grand Rapids, MI: Kregel, 1995, p. 30.

APPENDICES

Excursus One – Judas Iscariot: what's in a name?

1 Mark 3:13–19 (SV).
2 This was the common practice in the ancient world. The Hebrew word "Ben" and the Aramaic form "Bar" both mean "son of" and were in use during the time of Jesus, although the Aramaic form is found much more in the NT. It is interesting to note that in Mark 6:3 Jesus is identified in terms of his mother: "This is the son of the carpenter, isn't it? Isn't he Mary's son?" (SV). One interpretation of this is that Jesus' paternity was disputed – there is no mention of Joseph in Mark's gospel and Jesus is identified as a "carpenter" not "the carpenter's son," a detail Matthew changes (Mt 13:55). It could be that the lack of a (known? legitimate?) father in Jesus' life was a detail used to attack him. Again, scholars are unsure, but it is highly telling that Jesus is identified the way he is in Mark's gospel and that Matthew so noticeably changes the detail.
3 There is great debate among scholars as to exactly what the designate "zealot" means in relation to Simon. The Greek word *zēlotēs* (Hebrew root *qn'*) means one who is zealous (usually about God) and had been used in the Hebrew scriptures to describe those who were ardent in their efforts to protect God, e.g. Phineas (Num 25:6–13), the Maccabees (I Macc 2:24, 26) and, in the NT, to describe Paul's attachment to the traditions of his ancestors (Gal 1:13–14). However, there the Greek word *zēlotēs* was also used to describe a group of Jews, mostly young, who had vowed to fanatically protect the Law and Temple, and to attack any individuals who threatened their vision of a pure cultic center. From Josephus we hear of the Zealots becoming active only at the time of the First Jewish Revolt, in 67 CE; some scholars have attempted to establish a link between the Maccabeans of the second century BCE and the Zealots, thereby arguing that the latter group existed during the time of Jesus. E.P. Sanders argues that Barabbas, the criminal supposedly released in lieu of Jesus, displays the spirit on which the Zealots would later model themselves (*The Historical Figure of Jesus*, New York: Penguin Press, 1993, p. 190). Sanders ignores the most obvious understanding of Barabbas: the name "Bar" (son) and "Abbas" (Father) reveal the true meaning of the figure – the crowd has picked the wrong son of the Father, a detail the original listening audience would have understood easily. Furthermore there is no evidence that any criminals were released during festival time. Despite the debate surrounding the time in which the Zealots originally emerged, the group would have existed at the time Mark's gospel was formed, and the presence of Simon the Zealot may show that the group had an influence on the Markan community. We cannot know for sure, however, and any claims about Simon should be under-

stood as speculation. For a detailed discussion of the Zealots and the use of the Greek word *zēlotēs* in the scriptures, see Raymond Brown, *The Death of the Messiah: From Gethsemane to the Grave: A Commentary on the Passion Narratives in the Four Gospels*, 2 vols, New York: BantamDoubleday, 1994, pp. 689–93.

4 Notice that Levi, called in Mk 2:14 and in whose house Jesus dines in 2:15, is not named as one of the twelve. In fact, he disappears from the narrative entirely. I think it likely that Levi, like Bartimaeus in Mk 10:46–52, was a member of the Markan community.

5 William Klassen, *Judas: Betrayer or Friend of Jesus?* London: Augsburg Fortress, 1996, p. 29.

6 For a list of these see Klassen, op. cit., p. 30.

7 Hyam Maccoby, *Judas Iscariot and the Myth of Jewish Evil*, New York: Free Press, 1992, p. 5. While I disagree with much of the biblical exegesis done by Maccoby, the work is valuable in that it traces the perfidious growth of anti-Semitism through the Judas tradition. As such it is a worthwhile read; however, its glaring errors and poor biblical scholarship sharply undercut its efficacy. For a much better treatment of anti-Semitism in the overall Christian tradition, see James Carroll, *Constantine's Sword*, New York: Houghton Mifflin, 2001.

8 *Ennaratio in Ps 108*. 18, 20; CC 40. 1593, 1596; *Sermon 152*. 10; *Patrologia Latina* 38.824; taken here from Brown, op. cit., p. 1395.

9 Bonhoeffer's 17 March 1937 sermon entitled "Predigt am Sonntag Judika über Judas," in *Gessammelte Schriften*, pp. 406–13; taken here from Klassen, op. cit., p. 31.

10 See below item 1 in the discussion of "Iscariot" and my objection to this claim.

11 Brown, op. cit., p. 1411. There are literally dozens of theories about Judas' surname, discussion of which would be tedious and unnecessary for our purpose. For those who are interested in a detailed discussion, see Brown, op. cit., pp. 1410–16; and Klassen, op. cit., pp. 32–4.

12 Brown, op. cit., p. 1414.

13 Schwarz, pp. 6–12; cited in Brown, op. cit., p. 1414.

14 C.C. Torrey, "The Name 'Iscariot'." *HTR* 36 (1943): 51–62.

15 Klassen, op. cit., p. 32.

16 Brown, op. cit., p. 1415.

17 Flavius Josephus, *Antiquities*, trans. Louis H. Feldman, Cambridge: Loeb Classical Libraries, 1965, 20.8.10, pp. 186–7; and Flavius Josephus, *The Jewish War*, trans. by H.St.J. Thackery, Cambridge: Loeb Classical Libraries, 1967, 7.8.1; pp. 254–8.

18 Brown writes: "Only by anachronistic analogy does Josephus mention them [the Sicarii] earlier, in relation to the revolt in AD 6 by Judas the Galilean against the census of Quirinius. He never mentions them in the period of Pilate under Tiberius" (op. cit., p. 689; for a full discussion of the political scene and the various active groups, see pp. 679–93). Crossan, however, disagrees with Brown, arguing that the evidence in *Antiquities* is a revision of the earlier data in *War*, and claims that the Sicarii were responsible for the death of the high priest Jonathan (36 or 37 CE), the event Brown feels is attributed to the Sicarii anachronistically. Crossan concludes that "one could imagine the Sicarii operative for almost seventy years"

(John Dominic Crossan, *The Historical Jesus: The Life of a Mediterranean Jewish Peasant*, San Francisco: HarperCollins, 1992, p. 122; for a full treatment of Judas the Galilean and the Sicarii, see pp. 117–23).

While the issue is highly nuanced, I ultimately side with Brown in determining that Judas Iscariot was not a member of the Sicarii: "From the viewpoint of intelligibility, nothing in the described career of Judas in the NT would encourage one to think of him as a political revolutionary who would deserve this title" (Brown, p. 1415). As the title "Iscariot" is one that must be given anachronistically, and therefore not a family name, it seems unlikely from what we know of Judas that he was a member of the Sicarii, even if they were active at the time of Jesus.

As a final note, I find that John Shelby Spong overstates Crossan's case, and I regard as curious his claim "that the disciple band was armed with swords also suggests this possibility [that there were revolutionaries in Jesus' group] rather overtly . . . [but the] point is certainly not established. It is only hinted" (*Liberating the Gospels: Reading the Bible with Jewish Eyes*, San Francisco: HarperCollins, 1996, p. 43). How is it that being a disciple and carrying a sword are mutually exclusive? That one bears the typical arm used for defense in a rather violent and hostile world does not indicate that one is therefore a political revolutionary; to point out that this detail is hinted at does little more than fuel unnecessary speculation.

19 Klassen, op. cit., p. 33.
20 Ibid., p. 34.

Excursus Two – Judas as an historical figure

1 John Meier, *A Marginal Jew*, vol. 3, New York: Random House, 2001, p. 142.
2 Ibid., p. 143.
3 Ibid., p. 143.
4 Ibid., p. 143.
5 Ibid., p. 145.

Bibliography

Books

Alvarez, A., *The Savage God: A Study of Suicide*. New York: Random House, 1970.

Anderson, Janice Capel and Stephen D. Moore, *Mark and Method: New Approaches in Biblical Studies*. Minneapolis: Augsburg Fortress, 1992.

Augustine of Hippo, *Concerning the City of God, Against the Pagans*, translated by Henry Bettenson. New York: Penguin Books, 1984.

——, *Confessions*, translated by R.S. Pinecoffin. New York: Penguin Books, 1961.

Brown, Raymond E., *The Death of the Messiah: From Gethsemane to the Grave: A Commentary on the Passion Narratives in the Four Gospels*, 2 vols. New York: BantamDoubleday, 1994.

Calvin, John, *Harmony of the Evangelists*. Grand Rapids, MI: Baker Books, 2002.

Camus, Albert, *The Myth of Sisyphus: And other Essays*, translated by Justin O'Brien. New York: Vintage Books, 1955.

Carroll, James, *Constantine's Sword: The Church and the Jews, A History*. New York: Houghton Mifflin, 2001.

Crossan, John Dominic, *The Historical Jesus: The Life of a Mediterranean Jewish Persant*. San Francisco: HarperCollins, 1992.

——, *Who Killed Jesus: Exposing the Roots of Anti-Semitism in the Gospel Story of the Death of Jesus*. San Francisco: HarperCollins, 1996.

——, *The Birth of Christianity: Discovering What Happened in the Years Immediately After the Execution of Jesus*. San Francisco: HarperCollins, 1998.

Dibelius, Martin, *From Tradition to Gospel*, translated by Bertram Lee Woolf. New York: Charles Scribner's Sons, 1935.

Droge, Arthur J. and James D. Tabor, *A Noble Death: Suicide and Martyrdom Among Christians and Jews in Antiquity*. San Francisco: HarperCollins, 1992.

Durant, Will, *Caesar and Christ*, New York: Simon and Schuster, 1944.

Edwards, Richard A., *A Theology of Q*, Philadelphia: Fortress Press, 1976.

Harris, Stephen L., *The New Testament: A Student's Introduction*, 4th edn. New York: McGraw Hill, 2002.

Josephus, Flavius, *The Jewish War*, translated by H.St.J. Thackery. Cambridge: Loeb Classical Libraries, 1967.

——, *Jewish Antiquities*, translated by Louis H. Feldman. Cambridge: Loeb Classical Libraries, 1965.

Kealy, Sean P., *Mark's Gospel: A History of Its Interpretation*, Ramsey, NJ: Paulist Press, 1982.

Klassen, William, *Judas: Betrayer or Friend of Jesus?* London: Augsburg Fortress, 1996.

Kloppenborg, et al., *The Critical Edition of Q*. Minneapolis: Lewen/Fortress Press, 2000.

Maccoby, Hyam, *Judas Iscariot and the Myth of Jewish Evil*. New York: Free Press, 1992.

Mack, Burton L., *The Lost Gospel: The Book of Q and Christian Origins*. San Francisco: HarperCollins, 1993.

Meier, John, *A Marginal Jew*, vol. 3. New York: Random House, 2001.

Miller, Robert J. (ed.), *The Complete Gospels: Annotated Scholar's Version*, 3rd edn. Santa Rosa, Sonoma, CA: Polebridge Press, 1994.

Mishima, Yukio, *Patriotism*, translated by Geoffery W. Sergant. New York: New Directors, 1995.

Morrison, Frank, *Who Moved the Stone?*. London: Faber, 1930.

Nicolson, Adam, *God's Secretaries: The Making of the King James Bible*, New York: HarperCollins, 2003.

Pagels, Elaine, *The Origin of Satan*. New York: Random House, 1995.

Pavese, Cesare, *The Burning Brand: Diaries, 1935–1950*, New York: Walker, 1961.

Placher, William C., *A History of Christian Theology: An Introduction*. Philadelphia: Westminster Press, 1983.

——, *Readings in the History of Christian Theology, Volume One: From Its Beginnings to the Eve of the Reformation*. Philadelphia: Westminster Press, 1988.

Sanders, E.P., *The Historical Figure of Jesus*. New York: Penguin Press, 1993.

Schweitzer, Albert, *The Quest of the Historical Jesus: A Critical Study of Its Progress From Reimarus to Wrede*, 4th edn. New York: Macmillan, 1948.

Spong, John Shelby, *Liberating the Gospels: Reading the Bible with Jewish Eyes*. San Francisco: HarperCollins, 1996.

Tzu, Lao, *The Way of Life*, translated by Witter Bynner, New York: Perigree Books, 1944.

Wiersbe, Warren W. (ed.), *Classic Sermons on Judas Iscariot*, Grand Rapids, MI, Kregel, 1995.

Articles

Boyle, Peter J., "The Jesus war," *New Yorker*, 15 September 2003: 66–7.

Dewey, Arthur J., "Can we let Jesus die?" from *The Once and Future Faith*, Santa Rosa, Sonoma, CA: Polebridge Press, 2001.

Miller, Robert J., "Is the Apocalyptic Jesus history?" from *The Once and Future Faith*, Santa Rosa, Sonoma, CA: Polebridge Press, 2001.

Index

DAT